A 90-DAY DEVOTIONAL

POWER
UP!

Spiritual Nuggets for a Victorious Life

PASTOR AL BRICE

HIGHERLIFE

PUBLISHING & MARKETING

Printed in the United States of America
First Printing, 2020
ISBN 978-1-951492-76-2

Covenant Love Church
420 Dunn Road
Fayetteville, NC 28312
www.mycl.church

Acknowledgments

First and foremost, I thank my Heavenly Father for sending His greatest gift, His Son Jesus, to redeem me and bring me into a son relationship with Him. His revealed love, grace, and mercy have revolutionized my life.

I thank my amazing Lord and Savior, Jesus Christ. He gave me His salvation and a brand-new life to serve humanity.

I thank the Holy Spirit for leading me into Truth and helping me achieve every dream given to me by my Heavenly Father.

I want to give special thanks to my precious and faithful wife, Tava. She has truly been the greatest encouraging factor in my life, along with the Holy Spirit within me. She constantly inspires and cheers me on to greater accomplishments for the Kingdom of God. She has always picked me up when I'm facing difficult circumstances, and she speaks the Word of God over me by reminding me who God is to me, how He sees me, and how much He loves me. Her sense of humor always keeps me laughing when everything in me wants to cry at times. She is the greatest gift given to me outside my salvation and the Holy Spirit.

I also want to thank all our children for loving me unconditionally and allowing me to make mistakes without any condemnation. They are, along with our grandchildren, the apple of my eye.

I want to thank our incredible staff and the congregation at Covenant Love Church for being the best family, outside my biological family. They are a great source of encouragement to me and true intercessors for us.

I want to thank all our many friends and partners, in the Lord, who so faithfully give of their time and finances to help us achieve and accomplish all that we have been able to do for the Kingdom of God.

I especially want to thank my publishing assistant, Crisie Hutchings, who collaborated with me in writing this devotional. I appreciate all the hard work she contributed to the project. Thank you, Crisie.

Contents

CONTENTS

Foreword

HOW IMPORTANT IS DEVOTIONAL consistency in a believer's life? I personally have realized that the answer to this question determines the effectiveness of my life daily and the lives of so many. Daily devotional consistency in a believer's life is essential to his or her being able to walk in victory and in the power of The Holy Spirit.

At a time when time is everyone's greatest commodity, Pastor Al gives us both a weapon and a tool to defeat the lies of the enemy and jump-start our devotional walk with God in just a few minutes daily. These nuggets of wisdom will challenge your growth and reveal your true identity in Christ. Through this 90-day journey, you will discover who you are in Christ and who Christ is in you—what you were created for. You will understand that fear has no place where perfect Love resides, and you will learn that God gives us His best by us walking in obedience to His Word.

So, get ready for a journey of transformation that will lead you to Christ in a way that you may have not known and to a God that is committed to your success daily!

PASTOR SCOTT SCHATZLINE
Lead Pastor, Daystar Family Church
Northport, Alabama

ARE YOU WILLING TO run, walk, or even crawl back to the place where your freedom awaits? If you are, then this powerful 90-day devotional by my spiritual father, Pastor Al Brice, is for you. I have never met anyone who walks in wisdom, authority, purpose, and integrity like Pastor Al. God has used him to help guide our lives for almost two decades in a powerful and profound way. Now you, too, will be able to sit under the same tutelage as me and thousands of others, by reading his book.

This book is long overdue. It has marinated in Pastor Al's spirit and been bathed in prayer for years. I am reminded of a quote by Martin Luther, who once said, "If you want to change the world, pick up your pen and write." That is exactly what Pastor Al Brice has done with this book. Get prepared to be stirred and strengthened by every page! This book will take you on an adventure in faith, freedom, authority, wisdom, blessing, and identity. Every single page will stir your heart for more of Jesus! It reminds us all that the knock at the door of our spirits is not another opportunity to exalt self, but rather the knock of a victorious Savior calling us to live more deeply in *Him*! Jesus is saying, "Come to me, all you who are weary and burdened, and I will give you rest." (Matthew 11:28)

I believe this book is destined to be a classic. It reminds each of us that God is waiting for us to dust off the altars of encounter and enter the Most Holy Place.

This book also reminds each of us that we are the ones God wants to use to change the world. Your response to God will always determine the future of your family and your "*glo-cal*" circle of influence (the world in your backyard). It is time to be accountable to your *dash*! What is your dash? It is the line that someday will appear between your birth date and death date on your tombstone. We must make our dashes count! We are called to be overcomers! That means no more licking the wounds of past pain and rejection! Will you step into your destiny?

I believe now, more than ever, it is time for the bride of Christ to do as the Prophet Isaiah said: "Cry aloud and Spare not!" (Isa. 58:1) We must change the narrative being espoused from those who preach only from memories of yesterday's glory, not the humility and aroma of a most recent encounter with a Lamentations 3:23 "new every morning"

Savior! We must determine that our cries for *revival* matter more than the retribution of the religiously satisfied and the voices of lost holiness. Your voice matters now more than ever! Will you speak up? Dare we say to our kids that our nation was destroyed because we who had a voice decided the price to speak was costlier than their freedom? Will they look back and declare that "they" were loud for the wrong reasons and cowardice in the right season? I say, "*No!*" Let history speak of us as those who chose holiness over heathenism and purpose over procrastination.

This is our now! Pastor Al has written down the revelation, and now we must "run with it" (Hab. 2:2). We must rise up and lead a Holy Spirit revolution.

PATRICK H. SCHATZLINE
Evangelist and Author
Cofounder, Remnant Ministries International

Introduction

WE ARE LIVING IN trying and stressful times. We are seeing an escalation of evil and immorality like never before in our lifetime. The intensity of the kingdom of darkness has grown from year to year. The Apostle Paul warned us of these days:

"But know this, that in the last days perilous times will come: For men will be lovers of themselves, lovers of money, boasters, proud, blasphemers, disobedient to parents, unthankful, unholy, unloving, unforgiving, slanderers, without self-control, brutal, despisers of good, traitors, headstrong, haughty, lovers of pleasure rather than lovers of God, having a form of godliness but denying its power. And from such people turn away!"
—2 Timothy 3:1-5

How do we stand, keep on standing, and continue to walk in the victory given to us by Jesus Christ our Lord? By standing on the foundation of the Word of God!

"Therefore whoever hears these sayings of Mine, and does them, I will liken him to a wise man who built his house on the rock: and the rain descended, the floods came, and the winds blew and beat on that house; and it did not fall, for it was founded on the rock. But everyone who hears these sayings of Mine, and does not do them, will be like a foolish man who built his house on the sand: and the rain descended, the floods came, and the winds blew and

beat on that house; and it fell. And great was its fall."
—Matthew 7: 24-27

That is the purpose of this devotional: to build you up, encourage you, strengthen you, and to declare faith and hope to you so you can withstand the assaults of the powers of darkness. It will help you to keep walking through the valley times of life and overcome the trials and tribulations we all face in these trying times.

This devotional is like a lighthouse amid the storm, guiding you into a safe harbor of refuge. It instructs you on how to handle certain issues and includes a daily prayer for each addressed subject. The ninety nuggets of spiritual wisdom guide you, day by day.

My prayer is that it will help you and others for a long time and that you would encourage others to read God's Word each day and meditate on it.

Doing so will provide you with strength and comfort. As I look at the realities of chaos, confusion, fear, and uncertainty in our world today, I also see these issues seeping into the church. As sons and daughters of God, we must continually and constantly feed ourselves with the Word of God, which is our source of faith, confidence, and power.

"Who being the brightness of His glory and the express image of
His person, and upholding all things by the word of His power..."
—Hebrews 1:3

It's time to "power up" and advance into the future with strength and confidence derived from knowing His Word and claiming His promises!

Day 1

Do Not Fear

"For God has not given us a spirit of fear, but of power and of love and of a sound mind."
—2 Timothy 1:7

WHY ARE WE TOLD repeatedly in God's Word, "Do not fear"? Jesus told us in Matthew 6:25–34, *"Do not worry about your life, what you will eat or what you will drink; nor about your body, what you will put on…Therefore do not worry about to-morrow…"* Why would God make such a statement? Does He not realize what kind of world we are living in? Does He not understand the day-to-day issues and problems we face?

Yes, He does. In fact, He has already been in your tomorrow and knows everything you are going to face *before* you are confronted. He knows what your needs will be, and He has the wisdom and provision already waiting to meet those needs!

> *"Remember the former things of old,*
> *For I am God, and there is no other;*
> *I am God, and there is none like Me,*
> *Declaring the end from the beginning,*

And from ancient times things *that are not* yet *done,*
Saying, 'My counsel shall stand,
And I will do all My pleasure."
—Isaiah 46:9-10

God has declared His desired *end* for your situation at the *beginning* of your circumstance! He fulfills the promises He has already declared and spoken through His Word—the Bible.

So, what is your part? Job 22:28 gives us a clue: *"You will also declare a thing, and it will be established for you, so light will shine on your ways."* You must come into agreement with Him! Declare the portions of His Word that pertain to your situation, and He will fulfill His Word by performing the promises you have declared.

This is a promise in His Word, Jeremiah 1:12, from the Amplified Bible (AMP): *"Then the LORD said to me, 'You have seen well, for I am [actively] watching over My word to fulfill it.'"*

The moment you declare your prayer and continue to declare it, you, in agreement with Him, are declaring the end, from the beginning! You power up through prayer! Stop complaining and murmuring, and start declaring. Then watch God's will manifest with good results! It might not happen overnight, but what you wish for will manifest—that is called faith and patience.

> ### Prayer:
> Father, so many times I get my eyes on my circumstances and become fearful. Forgive me, and help me to see that you have gone before me. Lead me in your Word to understand and see that you have, indeed, gone before me in everything I may encounter—not only today, but tomorrow and every day of my life. Thank you for your love and care for me, and help me continually trust your Word and provision. I will declare your Word and promise over my life and watch as you perform it! Thank you, Father. In Jesus's name, amen.

Day 2

Standing Down

"Therefore take up the whole armor of God, that you may be able to withstand in the evil day, and having done all, to stand firm. Stand therefore..."
—Ephesians 6:13-14 (ESV)

AS SOLDIERS IN GOD'S army, we must always "stand up." Nowhere in Scripture are we instructed to "lay down our arms" or to "stand down"—to relax from a state of alertness—when it comes to our ongoing battle with the world, the flesh, and the devil. This is clearly expressed in the following Scriptures:

"For whatever is born of God overcomes the world. And this is the victory that has overcome the world—our faith."
—1 John 5:4

"Therefore put to death your members which are on the earth: fornication, uncleanness, passion, evil desire, and covetousness, which is idolatry."
—Colossians 3:5

"Be sober, be vigilant; because your adversary the devil walks
about like a roaring lion, seeking whom he may devour.
Resist him, steadfast in the faith…"
—1 Peter 5:8-9

Today and every day, take your stand—stand up for Jesus and righteousness! If you stand down, the enemies of your soul will bring sure destruction into your life. Stand up, power up, persevere, endure, overcome, and be a difference maker. Ephesians 6:17 says, *"And take the helmet of salvation, and the sword of the Spirit, which is the word of God."* Make sure you use your sword—the Word of God—in every circumstance you face.

You use the sword by speaking the Word of God with your mouth! Remember, you have God-given and delegated spiritual authority, but you must use it. Matthew 16:19 says, *"And I will give you the keys of the kingdom of heaven, and whatever you bind on earth will be bound in heaven, and whatever you loose on earth will be loosed in heaven."*

Prayer:

Thank you, Father, that you have given me authority and power over the wicked one. You have given me courage to *stand up*—and not only that, but to defeat every enemy. Thank you that your Spirit is alive in me so I can stand as David did, when he met Goliath and declared the enemy's demise! I take a stand against every mountain in my life, in faith, knowing that you have already defeated the devil, and all I have to do is trust and *stand*. Thank you, Father! In Jesus's name, amen.

Day 3

Prophecy...The Difference between Victory and Defeat

"And when the Philistine looked about and saw David, he disdained him; for he was only a youth, ruddy and good-looking. So the Philistine said to David, 'Am I a dog that you come to me with sticks?' And the Philistine cursed David by his gods. And the Philistine said to David, 'Come to me, and I will give your flesh to the birds of the air and the beasts of the field!' Then David said to the Philistine, 'You come to me with a sword, with a spear, and with a javelin. But I come to you in the name of the LORD of hosts, the God of the armies of Israel, whom you have defied. This day the LORD will deliver you into my hand, and I will strike you and take your head from you. And this day I will give the carcasses of the camp of the Philistines to the birds of the air and the wild beasts of the earth, that all the earth may know that there is a God in Israel. Then all this assembly shall know that the LORD does not save with sword and spear; for the battle is the Lord's, and He will give you into our hands.'"

—I Samuel 17:42–47

THE SCRIPTURE ABOVE SHOWS a life-changing principle that so many Christians have forgotten or don't know. It is the difference between victory and defeat. It is the story of David and Goliath, both prophesying to each other. One of the definitions of *prophecy* is to make inspired declarations of what we are believing now and what is to come. Job 22:28 says, *"You will also declare a thing and it will be established for you; so light will shine on your ways."* Romans 12:6 says, "Let us prophesy in proportion to our faith." David prophesied about his problem according to his faith in God's Word in verses 45-47.

Are you allowing your circumstances to prophesy your future and surrendering to them? Or are you prophesying and declaring God's Word—His promises—to your circumstances? Don't let your past failures or present problems declare your future. Declare your future by declaring God's Word and His will for your tomorrow.

Don't remain silent! Prophesy today, and continue to declare, and it will be established. Wake up, Davids! You are anointed kings in the Kingdom. Power up! Arise and run to the battle—don't be afraid. If God is for you, who or what can be against you?

Prayer:

Lord, you have awakened my heart to your Truth today, that I *can* have victory over my situation. I can stand and prophesy your outcome and silence the enemy who is trying to prophesy my outcome. You have promised that the battle is yours and that you *are* the winning side! I stand in courage and strength on that promise and prophesy the *victory*! In Jesus's name, amen.

Day 4

Courage against the Odds

"Then Caleb quieted the people before Moses, and said, 'Let us go up at once and take possession, for we are well able to overcome it.' But the men who had gone up with him said, 'We are not able to go up against the people, for they are stronger than we.'"
—Numbers 13:30-31

THE TEST OF COURAGE comes when you are in the minority and negative voices are speaking doom and gloom. Courage doesn't mean the absence of fear but rather moving forward, with confidence in God, and declaring His Word.

The test of tolerance comes when you are at odds with the majority because of what God has said. Sometimes the courage to stand for what God has said cultivates schisms with those who have a weak backbone that causes them to have a negative jawbone! Our behavior is determined by what's in our hearts and the images we have of ourselves. The way you see and think about yourself can carry you to the heights of success and victory, or it can plunge you into the depths of defeat and despair.

You were created in the image of God, with Him and His Word on your side. You can't lose! Caleb had a delay in his destiny, but his courage and confession of faith ultimately brought him victory and possession of the promise. Numbers 14:24 tells us, *"But My servant Caleb, because he has a different spirit in him and has followed Me fully, I will bring into the land where he went, and his descendants shall inherit it."*

Be of great courage today! Power up! God is for you, not against you. (Rom. 8:31) Greater is He that is in you than he who is in the world. (1 John 4:4) Remember, the same Spirit that raised Jesus from the grave lives in you. (Rom. 8:11) You are stronger than you think! Be strong in the Lord and in the power of His might. Go with courage and conquer; He is with you.

Prayer:

Father, there are times when I see myself as small and unable to conquer because of things I believe about myself, based on the lies of the enemy or the words of others. But there is only one Truth and Word that counts—yours! Yours is the final say. Yours is the final declaration, and you say I am more than a conqueror. You say I can do all things through Christ! You say you will never leave me or forsake me. so I take up the sword of your Spirit and run into battle, for you are with me! I will not fear. In Jesus's name, amen.

The test of courage comes when you are in the minority.

Day 5

Courage during Opposition

"I've told you all this so that trusting me, you will be unshakable and assured, deeply at peace. In this godless world you will continue to experience difficulties. But take heart! I've conquered the world."
—John 16:33 (MSG)

DOORS OF OPPORTUNITY WILL open as we pray, seek, and knock in accordance with God's will. Matthew 7:7–8 instructs us, *"Ask, and it will be given to you; seek, and you will find; knock, and it will be opened to you. For everyone who asks receives, and he who seeks finds, and to him who knocks it will be opened."* But opportunity will remain just opportunity until you take action to do something with it. The moment you power up with courage and advance against your opposition, opportunity becomes a reality of your destiny—to receive what God has planned and you have dreamed of.

With every open door from God, there will come opposition from the kingdom of darkness. 1 Corinthians 16:9 (MSG) tells us, *"A huge door of opportunity for good work has opened up here. (There is also mushrooming opposition.)"*

Don't give up or think something is wrong with you because there is opposition. No! It's not what you're doing wrong but what you're doing right that is attracting opposition and adversaries! Endure, persevere, and obey the Word. Following through all the way to the end will be a testimony that will influence and affect the lives of many people.

"Do not, therefore, fling away your [fearless] confidence, for it has a glorious and great reward. compensation of reward.
For you have need of patient endurance [to bear up under difficult circumstances without compromising], so that when you have carried out the will of God, you may receive and enjoy to the full what is promised."
—Hebrews 10:35–36 (AMP)

Prayer:

Holy Father, there are times I grow weary during opposition. Sometimes it is so fierce that I think I can't stand another moment. But you are in my trouble with me. No matter what comes against me, you are my refuge and strong tower, the One who causes me to triumph! You are my confidence Lord, the one who trains my hands for war and wins the victory, Thank you, Father, for your faithfulness to uphold me in every onslaught, I will not fling away my confidence or lose heart. In Jesus's name, amen.

With every open door from God, opposition will always come from the kingdom of darkness.

Day 6

Those Who Fear the Darkness Have No Idea What the Light Can Do

"Fear not, for I am with you"
—Isaiah 43:5 (ESV)

FEAR PRODUCES DREAD AND puts us into a heightened level of emotions. Being in that state causes us to react in ways that can eventually be detrimental to our well-being and the well-being of others.

Making decisions based on feelings of fear, that have no reality at the present time, caused by an evil spirit of fear, can produce an action that gives permission to the spirit of fear to bring into reality the very thing that we are fearing. Job 3:25–26 shows this truth: *"For the thing I greatly feared has come upon me, and what I dreaded has happened to me. I am not at ease, nor am I quiet; I have no rest, for trouble comes."*

Fear is a spiritual entity and must be dealt with through a greater spiritual power. This is confirmed in 2 Timothy 1:7: *"For God has not given us a spirit of fear, but of power and of love and of a sound mind."* And

He assures us in 1 John 4:4, "*You are of God, little children, and have over-come them, because He who is in you is greater than he who is in the world.*"

Fear wants you to stop, retreat, give up, hide, be confused, and start thinking that God is not going to help you or that God is the one who brought this situation you're now facing. Power up! Stand against the spirit of fear, confront it, and cast it out, along with all the thoughts that are contrary to God's Word and His love for you.

> *"There is no fear in love; but perfect love*
> *casts out fear, because fear involves torment.*
> *But he who fears has not been made perfect in love."*
> —1 John 4:18

Prayer:

Lord God, I come against the spirit of fear and cast it out, in Jesus's name! I renew my mind to your Word, God. I find that you have not given me fear, but you have given me love, power, and a sound mind. I thank you for the peace of God that surpasses all understanding and keeps my heart and my mind through Christ Jesus (Phil. 4:7). You have given me your peace—not as the world gives, but as Christ gives (John 14:27. I will let my heart be neither troubled nor afraid. In Jesus's name, amen.

Day 7

I Will Fear No Evil, for You Are with Me

"And now, brothers and sisters, we want you to know about the grace that God has given the Macedonian churches. In the midst of a very severe trial, their overflowing joy and their extreme poverty welled up in rich generosity."
—2 Corinthians 8:1-2 (NIV)

WE DO NOT NECESSARILY see the most revealing characteristics of true Christianity during times of comfort, prosperity, satisfaction, or ease, but rather in challenging times, persecutions, rejections, times of lack, trials and tests, controversy, circumstances beyond our own control, unexpected negative surprises, and an all-out assault from the kingdom of darkness.

Remember and recall God's promises to you in Jeremiah 1:19: *"They will fight against you, but they shall not prevail against you. 'For I am with you,' says the Lord, 'to deliver you.'"* And again, in Isaiah 35:4: *"Say to those who are fearful-hearted, 'be strong, do not fear! Behold, your God will come with vengeance, with the recompense of God; He will come and save you.'"*

Just like Jeremiah and the Apostle Paul, God will speak to you through His Word. He will tell you what is happening and what the outcome will be, because of who He is to you. Be strong and courageous, for your God goes before you. He is your rear guard and is with you wherever you go and in whatever you may face. He has not given us a spirit of fear but of power, love, and a sound mind. So power up, and fear no evil!

We learn in 2 Corinthians 1:9–10, *"Yes, we had the sentence of death in ourselves, that we should not trust in ourselves but in God who raises the dead, who delivered us from so great a death, and does deliver us; in whom we trust that He will still deliver us..."*

Prayer:

Father, I know that trials will come. I know that at times, it will feel like death is looming, but I will not fear, for you are *always* with me! You never leave me alone, and I never walk through any trial without you by my side. I thank you for this comfort, and knowing this gives me the strength to endure. Father, I bless you for your grace that is sufficient in my weakest moments. You will never let me go! You are a good, good Father! In Jesus's name, amen.

Day 8

Thanks Be to God...
He Gives Us the Victory

"But thanks be to God, who gives us the victory through our Lord Jesus Christ. There-fore, my beloved brethren, be steadfast, immovable, always abounding in the work of the Lord, knowing that your labor is not in vain in the Lord."
—1 Corinthians 15:57-58

REMEMBER, YOUR STARTING POINT in any battle will determine your outcome. Your starting point is always "in Christ"; therefore, you are starting with victory! You're not trying to get the victory; you already have victory when you start. *"But thanks be to God, who gives us the victory through our Lord Jesus Christ."* (1 Corin. 15:57)

"In Christ" also means "in the Word of God." Your starting point is in Christ and in His Word. What promise, in God's Word, are you starting with and standing on?

If you're in Christ and the Word of God is your starting place, then you already have what you've asked for simply because you've prayed for it. This is the starting place for the fight of faith. You must identify your starting point and declare, "Victory is mine right now!" You've already overcome, and now you are declaring what's yours in Christ. The Scripture in 2 Corinthians 2:14 says, *"Now thanks be to God who always leads us in triumph in Christ, and through us diffuses the fragrance of His knowledge in every place."*

You start in victory, so therefore your outcome has already been settled in heaven and on this earth. His Word in 1 John 5:4–5 promises, *"For whatever is born of God overcomes the world. And this is the victory that has overcome the world—our faith. Who is he who overcomes the world, but he who believes that Jesus is the Son of God?"*

Power up by claiming the victory He has given you!

> ### Prayer:
> Father, you have prepared a place of victory for my life from the very foundation of the world. You have already overcome! And in that place, I stand, live, and move forward with confidence. Not that I need to obtain the victory, as I already have it. I need to advance from that place of victory. Father, who is like you? There is none in heaven and earth, and I praise you because of who you are! You are mighty and victorious in all your ways, and I love you! In Jesus's name, amen.

Your starting point in any battle will determine your outcome.

Day 9

Speak the Truth in the Face of the "Facts"

"And you shall know the truth, and the truth shall make you free."
—John 8:32

FACTS AND TRUTHS ARE completely different. Facts belong to the earthly realm, but truths belong to the supernatural and eternal realm—eternal truths always triumph over earthly facts. While facts are accurate in the realm of time, facts can also contradict the eternal Truth of God's Word!

You cannot allow yourself to embrace facts over truths—acknowledge facts if they are accurate, but refuse to allow them to rule over the Truth. Facts are subject to change when you believe and exercise Truth by praying and declaring Truth to the facts. Bind your mind to Truth, pray Truth, and declare Truth. Don't deny facts, but if you come into agreement with facts without embracing, believing, and declaring Truth, the facts will triumph. Truth will always overcome facts; the Truth can alter and change facts. Remember, you were a sinner—fact—but you be-

24

lieved and confessed the Truth, and *Truth* changed the fact by changing your situation. You went from sinner to saint because of Truth.

A centurion soldier had a servant in his house who was sick [fact], but he sought the Truth [Jesus] because he knew the Truth had the power to change the fact. Matthew 8:8 tells us, *"The centurion answered and said, 'Lord, I am not worthy that You should come under my roof. But only speak a word, and my servant will be healed.'"* Fact: his servant was sick; Truth: he believed the Truth had the power to change the fact of the matter and the fact of sickness was changed to healing.

His Word is Truth, and Truth has already won over every negative fact. Power up by declaring His Truth! Truth is your starting place in the face of facts. Truth guarantees you an expected outcome.

"But thanks be to God, who gives us the victory through our Lord Jesus Christ."
—1 Corinthians 15:57

> ### Prayer:
> Dear Father, there are many "facts" in my life that are contrary to the Truth, but I know your Truth trumps everything! The facts may be screaming loud, but your Word echoes throughout all eternity as done and finished! Thank you for your Truth, for upholding it, and that it endures forever. Other things may pass away, including the facts staring me in the face, but your Truth abides forever. In Jesus's name, amen.

Eternal truths always triumph over earthly facts.

Day 10

Keep Calm and Know Your Enemy

"Those also who seek my life lay snares for me; those who seek my hurt speak of destruction, and plan deception all the day long."
—Psalm 38:12

THIS SPEAKS OF THE operation of the kingdom of darkness. Remember what the Apostle Paul taught us in 2 Corinthians 2:11: *"Lest Satan should take advantage of us; for we are not ignorant of his devices."* Ignorance is based on a lack of knowledge, not on an understanding knowledge or a lack of application of knowledge. Hosea 4:6 says, *"My people are destroyed for lack of knowledge. Because you have rejected knowledge, I also will reject you from being priest for Me; because you have forgotten the law of your God, I also will forget your children."*

Lack of knowledge equals defeat, but understanding and applying knowledge of God's Word equals victory. Proverbs 24:5 says *"A wise man is strong, Yes, a man of knowledge increases strength..."*

Power up by being on guard every day!

In 1 Peter 5:8–9 (MSG), we are instructed, *"Keep a cool head. Stay alert. The Devil is poised to pounce and would like nothing better than to catch you napping. Keep your guard up. You're not the only ones plunged into these hard times. It's the same with Christians all over the world. So keep a firm grip on the faith..."*

Stay firm in your faith because God will always make a way for you to escape. Fight the good fight of faith. Remember, the fight is fixed, and you will win, so don't give in or give up!

Prayer:

Father, there are many things that come into my life that are so much bigger than me. When that happens, I am tempted to fear. The enemy bombards me with thoughts of defeat, but you have told me to keep a cool head and stay focused on you, to stand firm in my faith. My faith is rooted in you and everything you are. So today, as I face many adversaries, I lean on your Word and your strength to keep me steadfast and immovable. I know I am not alone in my trials because my brothers and sisters are experiencing the same things and because you are always with me! Thank you, Father. In Jesus's name, amen.

Day 11

Standing Strong

*"Indeed, the hour is coming, yes, has now come, that you will be scattered, each to his
own, and will leave Me alone. And yet I am not alone, because the Father is with Me."*
—John 16:32

REMEMBER, WHEN YOU FACE adversity and problems that look taller
than Mt. Everest, you're not facing them by yourself. God is not
just *with* you; He is *in* you! Hebrews 13:5b–6 tells us, *"For He
Himself has said, 'I will never leave you nor forsake you.' So we
may boldly say: 'The LORD is my helper; I will not fear. What can man do
to me?'"*

The Spirit of victory and triumph is within you—the Spirit of wisdom and might. The provision of God is available and just awaiting your
prayer. The grace of God will empower you to stand strong.

You're the strongest when you're the weakest! In 2 Corinthians 12:9
(AMPC), we are told, *"But He said to me, My grace (My favor and lov-
ing-kindness and mercy) is enough for you [sufficient against any danger
and enables you to bear the trouble manfully]; for My strength and power
are made perfect (fulfilled and completed) and show themselves most effective in [your] weakness.'"*

God is for you, not against you. Power up by rebuking the spirit of fear, casting out all doubt, standing tall, and declaring His Word, which is the sword of the Spirit!

> ### Prayer:
> Lord, I know troubles will come, and at times I will feel weak in facing them, but your Word has guaranteed that when I am weak, that is when I am the strongest! I thank you, right now, for an abundance of your grace to carry me through my circumstances. You have committed yourself to my success in all things, no matter how it looks to me. You have provided your Word, your name, and your Holy Spirit to ensure that I am upheld and that I overcome anything the world or the enemy throws at me. I am never alone! In Jesus's name, amen.

Day 12

Facing Your Giants

"These were born to the giant in Gath, and they fell by the hand of David and by the hand of his servants."
—1 Chronicles 20:8

YOU WILL FACE GIANTS in this life. Giant problems, giant adversity and giant circumstances will arise and confront you at times. But remember, 1 John 4:4 assures us, *"You are of God, little children, and have overcome them, because He who is in you is greater than he who is in the world."*

"Yet in all these things we are more than conquerors through Him who loved us."
—Romans 8:37

You do not face the giants in life alone; you face them with the Father, the Son, and the Holy Spirit. You are never alone in the fight of faith. Your sword is more powerful than any weapon the enemy has. You've got the Word of God! Stand firm, go straight ahead, and fear not because God is with you, in you, and for you.

Romans 8:31 confirms for us, *"What then shall we say to these things? If God is for us, who can be against us?"* The key to your victories is based on what you are saying to the issues you're facing and what you continue to say until your giant falls. Giants will speak failure and death, but God's Word speaks success and life. So power up by speaking in accordance with God's Word!

Prayer:

Dear Lord, what am I to say to the things that come against me? If you are for me, it doesn't matter who or what's against me because you are greater than *all*, and you live in me! Lord, help me to have a revelation of that Truth—that you are greater in me than anything I face. Forgive me for the times when I feel like I face the world alone and act like it, too. Forgive me for allowing defeatist thinking instead of embracing the Truth that you are all I need. I turn to you! I depend on you and not my own strength or wisdom. I turn to you alone for the victory! In Jesus's name, amen.

Day 13

Boldness in the Face of Darkness

"For the kingdom of God is not in word but in power."
—1 Corinthians 4:20

THERE IS A DESPERATE cry from segments of the Body of Christ for the manifestation of power of God with signs, wonders, and miracles. With so many churches structuring their services like a fast-food drive-through restaurant, there is no room for a move of God or a demonstration of the power of the Holy Spirit.

Mark 16:20 says, *"And they went out and preached everywhere, the Lord working with them and confirming the word through the accompanying signs. Amen."* If we preach the Word, we must desire to see accompanying signs. People desire not only to hear the Word of God, but also to see the demonstration of the power of the Word.

We are facing a major aggressive move of the kingdom of darkness in our nation. We must pray like the apostles when faced with great opposition!

Acts 4:29–30 demonstrates the apostles' great dependence on the

Lord: *"Now, Lord, look on their threats, and grant to Your servants that with all boldness they may speak Your word, by stretching out Your hand to heal, and that signs and wonders may be done through the name of Your holy Servant Jesus."*

When there is proclamation, there must be time for confirmation and demonstration. We must be desperate to see the works of God, not the polished performance of human effort, or we will become like the Laodicea generation, the last of seven churches addressed in Revelation, which wavered in their commitments to the Christian faith! (See Rev. 3:14–22.)

Power up by being bold in the face of darkness!

Prayer:

Father, so often when we see darkness overcoming the world, we can begin to doubt of your Word and the things you have promised. Forgive us, Lord, when we don't look to your power and provision, when we try to do things in our own strength and effort, and when we look to ourselves and our own wisdom to accomplish what only you can by your Spirit. Turn the tide on the earth as we turn our hearts and expectations back to you, Lord, and away from our own devices. Give us the boldness to speak. I pray that you would stretch out your hand to heal our land, and that signs, wonders, and miracles may be done through the mighty name of Your Holy Servant, Jesus. Heal our land, and heal our nation in Jesus's name, amen.

We must be desperate to see the works of God—not the polished performance of human effort—or we will become like the Laodicea generation.

Day 14

Going Forward in Faith

"Brethren, I do not count myself to have apprehended; but one thing I do, forgetting those things which are behind and reaching forward to those things which are ahead, I press toward the goal for the prize of the upward call of God in Christ Jesus."
—Philippians 3:13-14

REVERSE IS USED TO back out of a place that restricts or prohibits us from going forward, but then we must drive forward. If you continue to look in the rear-view mirror of the past, you will eventually crash and become unable to move forward, which is what you were created to do. There is a reason that God put our eyes in the front of our heads, not the back of our heads!

The enemy will do everything he can to stop you from advancing, but the only person who can stop you from going forward in life is you. Yes, tough times, testing, offenses, and personal attacks will come, but everything that comes to you also comes to the Spirit of God that is in you!

He will give you wisdom to make the right decisions—just ask. His grace and power will carry you forward, but you must put the feet to it in faith.

"And the LORD said to Moses, 'Why do you cry to Me? Tell the children of Israel to go forward. But lift up your rod and stretch out your hand over the sea and divide it.' And the children of Israel shall go on dry ground through the midst of the sea."
—Exodus 14:15-16

Power up by going forward—not in your strength, but in His strength—and see what miracle awaits you!

> ### *Prayer:*
> Father, so many times I get my eyes on the past—pain, failures, and disappointments. These keep me from going forward and keep me from your best. Lord, give me the wisdom I need to make right decisions and the power to go forward when my past is screaming in my mind. Help me to remember all the things you have done and the things you have promised to do in my life! I set my face like flint to go forward in your love and purpose! In Jesus's name, amen.

Reverse is used to back out of a place that restricts or prohibits us from going forward.

Day 15

Living from the Victory

"But thanks be to God, who gives us the victory through our Lord Jesus Christ."
—1 Corinthians 15:57

WE DON'T PRAISE THE Lord just for victory to come because He's already given us victory over every situation at the beginning. Therefore, we praise Him for the victory that He has already secured for us. And as we do it, by faith, we will see the manifestation of the victory that He has already promised us in His Word!

Joshua 6:2 declares, *"And the LORD said to Joshua: 'See! I have given Jericho [victory] into your hand, its king, and the mighty men of valor'"* (I added the word "victory" for clarification.) You must see by faith what God has already given you before you step out in faith. Faith is not a blind leap! How was Joshua able to see the victory before he applied action? Because God said, "I have given."

What has God given to you? In 2 Peter 1:4, His Word says, *"By which have been given to us exceedingly great and precious promises, that through these you may be partakers of the divine nature, having escaped the corruption that is in the world through lust."*

And 1 John 5:4 says, *"For whatever is born of God overcomes the world. And this is the victory that has overcome the world—our faith."*

It's our responsibility to fight the good fight of faith. Power up by declaring His Promises and the giving of praise, until you see the manifestation of what you are believing!

> *"Yours, O LORD, is the greatness, the power and the glory,*
> *the victory and the majesty; for all that is in heaven and*
> *in earth is Yours; Yours is the kingdom, O LORD,*
> *And You are exalted as head over all."*
> —1 Chronicles 29:11

Prayer:
Lord, I thank you that you have already given us victory over every situation. I praise you for the victory that is already mine in you! I praise you in faith that victory is mine, by and through your Word. In Jesus's name, amen.

It's our responsibility to fight the good fight of faith until we see the manifestation of what we are believing.

Day 16

If God Is for You

"The Lord will cause your enemies who rise against you to be defeated before your face; they shall come out against you one way and flee before you seven ways."
—Deuteronomy 28:7

YOU ARE MORE THAN a conqueror! No one and nothing can defeat you unless you first see yourself as defeated. The way you see yourself and your situation will determine your outcome. You must see yourself the way God sees you, and you must see your situation the way God sees it because you are one with Him. You must see Him and His Word as one. Both are working with and for you to have victory.

There is only one thing God cannot do: He cannot fail. If you doubt who you are in Christ and doubt God's ability in you and the promises He has given to you, that is like joining the enemy and bearing weapons against yourself. The only way the children of Israel experienced defeat was when they chose to believe what they saw versus what God said. The way you see yourself is the way you think your enemies see you.

Numbers 13:33 says, *"There we saw the giants (the descendants of Anak came from the giants); and we were like grasshoppers in our own sight, and so we were in their sight."* See yourself as God sees you: victorious and undefeatable. And Philippians 4:13 says, *"I can do all things through Christ who strengthens me."*

Power up by getting yourself back in faith. You're not defeated; you're only experiencing delayed victory—so don't give up! Galatians 6:9 encourages us: *"And let us not grow weary while doing good, for in due season we shall reap if we do not lose heart."*

Prayer:

Father, my eyes are on you. My faith is in you. All my expectations are in your victory that is already mine! I will not fear because you are with me, and you have promised that I will reap rewards if I do not lose heart. Lord, let my faith not fail me. Strengthen me to endure. In Jesus's name, amen.

Day 17

Don't Come Down Off the Wall

"Then the people of the land tried to discourage the people of Judah. They troubled them in building, and hired counselors against them to frustrate their purpose all the days of Cyrus king of Persia, even until the reign of Darius king of Persia."
—Ezra 4:4–5

AS YOU BUILD YOUR life in accordance with God's will, and begin to build your dreams, there will be opposition and obstacles. The devil will move in the hearts of people to discourage you. Not everyone will be happy about your endeavors and successes. People can be jealous and envious of your progress and can stir up negativity toward you.

In 1 Samuel 17:28–30, we learn about Eliab and David: *"Now Eliab his oldest brother heard when he spoke to the men; and Eliab's anger was aroused against David, and he said, 'Why did you come down here? And with whom have you left those few sheep in the wilderness? I know your pride and the insolence of your heart, for you have come down to see the battle.' And David said, 'What have I done now? Is there not a cause?' Then he turned from him toward another and said the same thing; and these people answered him as the first ones did."*

You must do like David: turn from the negative words that people speak! Embrace what God says you can do.

Don't get caught up in that trap of letting other people's opinions dampen your faith. Put it aside, and focus on where you're going with God. Stay busy with your dream, not with the voices of discouragement. Hebrews 10:35–36 (AMPC) instructs us, *"Do not, therefore, fling away your fearless confidence, for it carries a great and glorious compensation of reward. For you have need of steadfast patience and endurance, so that you may perform and fully accomplish the will of God, and thus receive and carry away [and enjoy to the full] what is promised."*

Power up by moving forward with God's purpose and plans for your life.

> ### Prayer:
> Father God, many there may be against me, but there is more with me than with them! Thank you for strengthening me to continue in the dreams and future you have for me, no matter what comes against me. You said no weapon formed against me can prosper (Isa. 54:17), so I will not worry what man can do to me. In Jesus's name, amen.

Not everyone will be happy about your endeavors and successes.

Day 18

The Power of the Word of God

"Let no one say when he is tempted, 'I am tempted by God'; for God cannot be tempted by evil, nor does He Himself tempt anyone. But each one is tempted when he is drawn away by his own desires and enticed. Then, when desire has conceived, it gives birth to sin; and sin, when it is full-grown, brings forth death."

—James 1:13–15

HOW DID JESUS OVERCOME every temptation of the devil in the wilderness? How did He resist the devil? With the Word of God. Luke 4:8 says, *"And Jesus answered and said to him, 'Get behind Me, Satan! For it is written, "You shall worship the Lord your God, and Him only you shall serve."'"*

He had read, studied, meditated, and memorized God's Word, and He hid it in His heart! Psalm 119:11 declares, *"Your word I have hidden in my heart, that I might not sin against You."*

When tempted, He spoke the Word immediately: "It is written." But we can't say, "It is written" if we don't know *what* is written. Power up by reading, studying, and memorizing the Word of God. It can save your life! Out of the abundance of your heart, your mouth will speak. Luke 6:45 *says, "A good man out of the good treasure of his heart brings forth* good; and an evil man out of the evil treasure of his heart brings forth evil. For out of the abundance of the heart his mouth speaks."

What is stored up in your heart?

> "My son, give attention to my words;
> Incline your ear to my sayings.
> Do not let them depart from your eyes;
> Keep them in the midst of your heart;
> For they are life to those who find them,
> And health to all their flesh.
> Keep your heart with all diligence,
> For out of it spring the issues of life."
> —Proverbs 4:20–23

Prayer:

Father, I thank you for your Word, which is the answer to every problem, the strength I need to walk in your ways, and the sword you have provided to slay the enemy. Thank you for the power of your Word. I pray to continue steadfast in it and to boldly speak it out of my mouth, always! In Jesus's name, amen.

Day 19

The Truth Never Changes

"There is a way that seems right to a man, but its end is the way of death."
—Proverbs 14:12

YOU CAN DENY OR suppress the Truth, but it doesn't change the Truth. Some people try to change and mold the Truth to fit into their lifestyles and cater to their own desires, but Truth will change our lifestyles and desires to be conformed into the image of Christ, who is the absolute Truth. God does not allow us to alter His Truth to fit into the way we want to live. He commands, not suggests, us to accept His Truth and to order our lives by being obedient to His Truth.

Beware of carnal believers who live destitute of the whole Truth. They will attempt to draw you away from obedience to the Truth. Galatians 3:1 says, *"O foolish Galatians! Who has bewitched you that you should not obey the truth...?"*

The only right way is obeying and living by God's Truth; He accepts nothing else. Psalm 33:4 says, *"For the word of the Lord is right, and all His work is done in truth."* The Truth set me free, and obeying the Truth keeps me free!

44

"And you shall know the truth, and the truth shall make you free."
—John 8:32

John 3:20–21 says, *"For everyone practicing evil hates the light and does not come to the light, lest his deeds should be exposed. But he who does the truth comes to the light, that his deeds may be clearly seen, that they have been done in God."*

Power up by embracing and living the Truth!

> **Prayer:**
> Father, I want to embrace and live the Truth! Your Word is perfect and has the power to transform my life and me. Forgive me for the times I pick and choose what governs my lifestyle instead of allowing the whole counsel of your Word to define and guide me. Strengthen my resolve to remain in your Truth. In Jesus's name, amen.

God does not allow us to alter His Truth to fit into the way we want to live.

Day 20

Stay Steadfast in the Truth

"Now the Spirit expressly says that in latter times some will depart from the faith, giving heed to deceiving spirits and doctrines of demons..."
—1 Timothy 4:1

"For the time will come when they will not endure sound doctrine, but according to their own desires, because they have itching ears, they will heap up for themselves teachers; and they will turn their ears away from the truth, and be turned aside to fables."
2 Timothy 4:3-4

THE HOLY SPIRIT DECLARES that in these last days, some in the church will not desire ideological purity, biblical holiness, and theological truth. Therefore, they will seek out a church and someone to listen to who is in the middle—someone who is tolerant, will bend with everyone else's beliefs, and will adopt the desires of the prevailing culture. The Scripture in 2 Timothy 4:10 says, *"For Demas has forsaken me, having loved the present world, and has departed for Thessalonica...."*

Please don't fall for this deception! Pursue holiness, embrace the truth of God's Word, and be the light in this present darkness. Philippians 2:15 says, *"That you may become blameless and harmless, children of God without fault in the midst of a crooked and perverse generation, among whom you shine as lights in the world...."*

Guard your heart, eyes, and ears, and stay on fire for Jesus! Proverbs 4:23 (NLT) instructs us, *"Guard your heart above all else, for it determines the course of your life."*

Your life and the lives of others are at stake. Power up, and stand up! Don't stand down, but be counted among the faithful, even if you're the only one. In the end, you'll hear, *"Well done, good and faithful servant..."* (Matt. 25:21).

Prayer:

Lord, there are many voices in the world vying for my ear and allegiance. But the only voice that matters is yours. The only allegiance I give is to you and your Word. Teach me, O Lord, the way of your statutes, and I shall keep them to the end. Give me understanding, and I shall keep your law; indeed, I shall observe it with my whole heart (Ps. 119:33–34). In Jesus's name, amen.

Day 21

What Are You Declaring?

"Nevertheless the Lord your God would not listen to Balaam, but the Lord your God turned the curse into a blessing for you, because the Lord your God loves you."
—Deuteronomy 23:5

TODAY AND EVERY DAY, the Word of God declares that you're blessed in the city and blessed in the field, blessed in your coming in and blessed in your going out. Jesus redeemed us from the curse of the law. Galatians 3:13–14 declares, *"Christ has redeemed us from the curse of the law, having become a curse for us (for it is written, 'Cursed is everyone who hangs on a tree'), that the blessing of Abraham might come upon the Gentiles in Christ Jesus, that we might receive the promise of the Spirit through faith."*

Instead of murmuring and complaining about certain circumstances or being concerned about someone trying to put a curse on you, start declaring what God has done and promised. Remember, what God has blessed, no one can curse, and you are blessed by God.

Does it make a difference to declare God's Word over you and your family? Job 22:28 promises, *"You will also declare a thing, and it will be established for you; so light will shine on your ways."*

Isaiah 44:8 says, *"Do not fear, nor be afraid; have I not told you from that time, and declared it?..."*

What are you declaring? Blessing or complaining, victim or victory, negativity or His Word? God is the only one who can turn your mess into a message and every test into a testimony. Power up by declaring His Word of blessing!

> **Prayer:**
> Dear Father, I have allowed the enemy to silence my confession of your Word and your Truth. I have been overwhelmed with the circumstances of life and used my voice to complain and murmur. I repent and turn my heart to seek your Word and to declare it, to take hold of your Word to declare what *you* have said about the circumstances and my life. In Jesus's name, amen.

God is the only One who can turn your mess into a message and every test into a testimony.

Day 22

Walking in the Supernatural

"And my speech and my preaching were not with persuasive words of human wisdom, but in demonstration of the Spirit and of power, that your faith should not be in the wisdom of men but in the power of God."
—1 Corinthians 2:4–5

HOLY SPIRIT, SHOW US today how to manifest your power and love to a hurting world.

To be blunt, Christianity is either supernatural or nothing at all. We had—and still have—a supernatural Jesus, with a supernatural ministry, creating a supernatural church, with a supernatural Gospel and a supernatural Bible. Take the miracle away, and you have taken Christianity's life away. The church becomes an ethical society, or a social club, when it is intended to be the grid system for transmitting the power of God into this powerless world.

> *"And these signs will follow those who believe: In My name they will cast out demons; they will speak with new tongues; they will take up serpents; and if they drink anything deadly, it will by no means hurt them; they will lay hands on the sick, and they will*

50

recover. So then, after the LORD had spoken to them, He was received up into heaven, and sat down at the right hand of God. And they went out and preached everywhere, the Lord working with them and confirming the word through the accompanying signs. Amen."
—Mark 16:17-20

You and I are conductors of God's power to the world! In John 14:12–14, Jesus promises us, *"Most assuredly, I say to you, he who believes in Me, the works that I do he will do also; and greater works than these he will do, because I go to My Father. And whatever you ask in My name, that I will do, that the Father may be glorified in the Son. If you ask anything in My name, I will do it."*

Power up by walking in the supernatural!

Prayer:

Father, thank you for bringing me into your unshakable Kingdom—a Kingdom of the supernatural. In my strength and ability, I am nothing, but you have given me your very own Spirit so I can accomplish the very same things that Jesus did when He walked this earth. His same authority is mine that same power lives in me. Thank you for entrusting this supernatural life to my charge. Help me be faithful and full of faith to walk in it. In Jesus's name, amen.

Day 23

The Calming Effect

"Lᴏʀᴅ, my heart is not haughty, nor my eyes lofty. Neither do I concern myself with great matters, nor with things too profound for me. Surely, I have calmed and quieted my soul, like a weaned child with his mother; Like a weaned child is my soul within me. O Israel, hope in the Lᴏʀᴅ from this time forth and forever."

—Psalm 131

IN THE SCRIPTURE ABOVE, King David was saying, in essence, "Lord, when things are too big for me to handle, when things are happening that I do not totally understand, the first thing I must do is calm and bring quietness to my mind." Your mind will run like a wild stallion that has been let loose if you do not bring it under control and back in alignment with who God is, how powerful He is, and how much He loves you. You can calm your mind by taking captive and rebuking thoughts that are contrary to His promises.

The Scripture in 2 Corinthians 10:3–5 declares, *"For though we walk in the flesh, we do not war according to the flesh. For the weapons of our warfare are not carnal but mighty in God for pulling down strongholds, casting down arguments and every high thing that exalts itself against the knowledge of God, bringing every thought into captivity to the obedience of Christ."*

And finally, David said, *"Hope in the Lord!"* The word *hope* means to trust and have patience. He will not let you down or disappoint you.

When you put on praise music and begin to declare His Word, that is The Calming Effect. Power up, and turn up the praise music!

"Trust in the LORD with all your heart and lean not on your own understanding; In all your ways acknowledge Him, And He shall direct your paths."
—Proverbs 3:5–6

> ### Prayer:
> Lord, just as King David did, I set my eyes on you and pray for your peace to envelop me. I pray you would quiet my soul. This situation is too big for me, so I come to you and rest in your presence. Thank you for your peace and calm during this situation right now. In Jesus's name, amen.

Your mind will run like a wild stallion that has been let loose if you don't bring it under control and back in alignment with who God is.

Day 24

What Are You Fixed On?

"O God, my heart is fixed (steadfast, in the confidence of faith); I will sing, yes,
I will sing praises, even with my glory [all the faculties and powers
of one created in Your image]!"
—Psalm 108:1 (AMPC)

YOU MUST FIX YOUR eyes, ears, mouth, and heart on what God's Word says about your issues. Then comes prayer, which must be a prayer of faith, which is based on God's promises.

Then comes praising and thanking God every day until you see results—not *re*-praying every day for the thing you prayed about. If I'm praying the same thing every day, concerning the same personal circumstances, then that means I didn't believe the first day. I am praising and thanking God every day for what I prayed for, according to His promises.

Philippians 4:6–7 tells us, *"Be anxious for nothing, but in everything by prayer and supplication, with thanksgiving, let your requests be made known to God; and the peace of God, which surpasses all understanding, will guard your hearts and minds through Christ Jesus."*

Power up by fixing your heart in faith. Faith comes by hearing God's promises, believing Him and His Word, and then continuing to *praise Him for your answer and declare His promise*!

"The LORD is my strength and my shield;
My heart trusted in Him, and I am helped;
Therefore my heart greatly rejoices,
And with my song I will praise Him."
—Psalm 28:7

> **Prayer:**
> Lord, thank you for always hearing me when I pray. Thank you for your Word that never fails in any circumstance I face. I trust you, I believe you, and I thank you that no matter what I see, your promise is sure in my life. In Jesus's name, amen.

If I keep on and keep on asking for the same thing I've already prayed for, then I didn't pray in faith to begin with.

Day 25

Focus

"You will keep in perfect and constant peace the one whose mind is steadfast [that is, committed and focused on You—in both inclination and character], because he trusts and takes refuge in You [with hope and confident expectation]. Trust [confidently] in the LORD forever [He is your fortress, your shield, your banner], for the LORD GOD is an everlasting Rock [the Rock of Ages].
—Isaiah 26:3-4 (AMP)

T IS SO EASY, in the age we live in, to get distracted from the Source of life and our Help in times of trouble. Fear and circumstances can scream loudly, intending to keep our focus away from God and His promises. We must cast down those distracting thoughts of doom and gloom and get our focus back on God and His Word. Praise and declaration of who He is and what He has promised will realign your focus, and peace will flood your heart.

If you think only about your problems, you will constantly be full of anxiety and worry. If you constantly think about the goodness of God and His promises, you will continue in peace of mind. Power up, and transform your negative thoughts into positive, God-filled thoughts!

"Finally, brethren, whatever things are true, whatever things are noble, whatever things are just, whatever things are pure, whatever things are lovely, whatever things are of good report, if there is any virtue and if there is anything praiseworthy— meditate on these things."
—Philippians 4:8

Prayer:

Father, the times we are living in are hard to bear sometimes. I get distracted and set my eyes on the hardship I'm going through instead of your Word. Please forgive me and strengthen me during this time. You are my fortress and shield! You are my everlasting Rock. I will confidently trust in you. In Jesus's name, amen.

Day 26

Silencing Your Enemies

"Lord, your name is so great and powerful! People everywhere see your splendor.
Your glorious majesty streams from the heavens, filling the earth with
the fame of your name!

You have built a stronghold by the songs of babies. Strength rises up with the chorus
of singing children." This kind of praise has the power to shut Satan's mouth.
Childlike worship will silence the madness of those who oppose you."
—Psalm 8:1-2 (TPT)

DID YOU KNOW THAT praise is a powerful weapon against the kingdom of darkness? When the voices of accusation, condemnation, negativity, doubt, and oppression start shouting at you, you must become louder with your praise! This kind of praise has the power to shut Satan's mouth. Childlike worship will silence the madness of those who oppose you.

Praise will shut the devil's mouth. Do not remain silent during his relentless verbal attack—*praise your God*! Doing so will cause the devil to have a nervous breakdown and will shut him up. He knows that when you praise your God, He will move against the devil and defeat his plans.

Do it now. Power up by moving past your negative emotions and shouting His praise!

Prayer:

I worship you, my heavenly Father, my mighty God! I proclaim your greatness, your mighty power. I believe in you and you alone. And today I choose to worship you in spirit and truth because you are faithful to your sons and daughters. You have never forsaken those who love and express their faith in you. I declare right now, in this situation, your glory and your majesty in the face of my circumstances. And I loudly announce right now that there is nothing impossible for you! I declare your goodness, grace, mercy, and kindness toward me because of the blood of Jesus, the everlasting covenant that you have made with us. My eyes are upon you, Almighty God, with great expectations because all your promises are *yes*, and I am saying the "amen!" In Jesus's name, amen.

Day 27

The Necessity of God's Word

"My people are destroyed for lack of knowledge..."
—Hosea 4:6

OUR GREATEST ENEMY IS not the devil, for he has been defeated. It is ignorance of God's Word and not knowing God. Knowing God comes through the reading and studying of His Word. Once you receive Jesus Christ as Lord of your life, then your mind, as a Christian, can be renewed only by God's Word. Faith can come into our lives only by the Word of God. The fruit of an active prayer life comes by the Word of God abiding in us.

John 15:7–8 says, *"If you abide in Me, and My words abide in you, you will ask what you desire, and it shall be done for you. By this My Father is glorified, that you bear much fruit; so, you will be My disciples."*

We're commanded to let the Word of God dwell in us in abundance. Colossians 3:16 says, *"Let the word of Christ dwell in you richly in all wisdom, teaching and admonishing one another...."*

The greatest deception is not actively doing what the Word of God commands us to do. James 1:22 instructs us, *"But be doers of the word, and not hearers only, deceiving yourselves."* What's hindering or distracting you from God's Word? It's time to take inventory of your time. Power up, and focus on making Him and His Word your number one priority!

> **Prayer:**
> Father, forgive me for allowing the distractions of my life to choke out my time with you in prayer and in your Word. I have felt the effects of it in my life, my heart, and my faith. Restore to me the passion I once had for your Word and your presence. Lead me in the paths of righteousness for your name's sake (Psalm 23). In Jesus's name, amen.

Your success will be determined by your prayer life and the depth of God's Word in your heart.

Day 28

Built upon the Rock

"Therefore whoever hears these sayings of Mine, and does them, I will liken him to a wise man who built his house on the rock: and the rain descended, the floods came, and the winds blew and beat on that house; and it did not fall, for it was founded on the rock. But everyone who hears these sayings of Mine, and does not do them, will be like a foolish man who built his house on the sand: and the rain descended, the floods came, and the winds blew and beat on that house; and it fell. And great was its fall."
—Matthew 7:24-27

WE MUST BUILD OUR lives on the rock of God's Word—not just by reading it or hearing it, but by doing it. Jesus said, "Whoever hears these sayings of mine and *does* them" will be the one who builds his house on a rock. What are you building your life on? If it's the world's ways, it will eventually collapse. But if you are building your life on Jesus and the Word of God, you will continue to stand, sing, and shout in the storm because He is your sure foundation, refuge, and shield. Power up, and build your life upon the rock!

In the uncertain days we live in, we cannot neglect to build our houses on the rock and keep on building. You never know when sudden calamity will come, but you can be assured that your house, your life, will stand when you build on the Rock of God's Word, no matter what comes! Circumstances cannot win with your foundation solidly built on your trust in God and His Word.

Prayer:

Father, I want to build my house on the rock of your Word—not just by hearing it, but by doing it. Forgive me for the times I have been complacent and took for granted your blessings and protection or have been apathetic to the importance of building my life in prayer, the study of your Word, and fellowship with you. I want to be steadfast and obedient to your voice! Strengthen me to continue in your Word and trust fully in it, no matter what the culture around me is saying and doing. In Jesus's name, amen.

Day 29

Keep Your Confidence

"Do not, therefore, fling away your [fearless] confidence, for it has a glorious and great reward. For you have need of patient endurance [to bear up under difficult circumstances without compromising], so that when you have carried out the will of God, you may receive and enjoy to the full what is promised."
—Hebrews 10:35–36 (AMP)

OUR CONFIDENCE IN GOD and in His Word must be undaunted. We must walk with endurance during this time in our history.

Hebrews 12:1–2 says, *"Therefore we also, since we are surrounded by so great a cloud of witnesses, let us lay aside every weight, and the sin which so easily ensnares us, and let us run with endurance the race that is set before us, looking unto Jesus, the author and finisher of our faith, who for the joy that was set before Him endured the cross, despising the shame, and has sat down at the right hand of the throne of God."*

We must not abandon our purpose, vision, mission, or dreams. We will persevere, fight the fight of faith, and overcome because we are the kings and priests of the Kingdom of God!

"For though we walk in the flesh [as mortal men], we are not carrying on our [spiritual] warfare according to the flesh and using the weapons of man. The weapons of our warfare are not physical [weapons of flesh and blood]. Our weapons are divinely powerful for the destruction of fortresses."
—2 Corinthians 10:3–4 (AMP)

We will not abandon our faith or our purposes. Yes, our methods may change, but our mission remains the same. Power up, and be strong in the Lord and the power of His might!

> ### *Prayer:*
> Dear God, these times are hard and pressing on us. In our flesh, we may feel weak, but in our spirit lives the same Spirit that raised Christ from the dead. I stand strong in your power! I stand because you are faithful over my life and have given me the Sword of the Spirit and a great armor so that I will not fall in the evil day, but having done all to stand...*I will stand*! In Jesus's name, amen.

Day 30

God Has Commanded Victory for You

"You are my King, O God;
Who commands victories for Jacob.
Through You we will push down our enemies;
Through Your name we will trample those who rise up against us."
—Psalm 44:4-5

GOD IS COMMANDING VICTORIES for you today and every day. Anything you face, face with confidence because at the very beginning, God commanded the victory in your favor. Notice, the Scripture above shows you your part in the victory.

We must come into agreement with that which He has commanded. Every thought contrary to what God has commanded, we must cast down and continue to move forward with praise and declare His promises. Power up by claiming God's victory for your life!

If we become double-minded, wavering back and forth between doubt and belief, we negate what has been commanded. Stay in agreement with your faith, with what God has commanded!

*"But thanks be to God, who gives us the victory
through our Lord Jesus Christ."*
—1 Corinthians 15:57

*"What then shall we say to these things,
If God is for us, who can be against us?"*
—Romans 8:31

> **Prayer:**
> Jesus, you are Captain of the Armies of the Lord! You *are* the victory! And because of that, I have every victory. Forgive me when I speak contrary to your victory; order my conversation to bring it into agreement with your command. Your victory is sure because you are the Resurrection and the Life. You have already defeated the enemy once and for all and for all eternity! In Jesus's name, amen.

Anything you face, face with confidence because at the very beginning, God has commanded the victory in your favor.

Day 31

Holding Fast to His Promises

"Let us hold fast the confession of our hope without wavering,
for He who promised is faithful."
—Hebrews 10:23

WHEN WE PRAY, THERE is usually a time lapse between the asking and the manifestation of the receiving. This is the time when the devil does everything possible to make us believe that our prayers will not be answered. I call this period "the fight of faith."

The verse above tells us to hold fast the confession of our hope (faith) without wavering. The statement "without wavering" refers to something that does not bend or break, something that is fixed and unmoving, and is therefore deep-rooted, enduring, and steadfast. A person who is without wavering is the opposite of one who easily succumbs to circumstances, throws in the towel, and has a give-up attitude.

"Without wavering" declares an attitude of unbending, unchanging, fixed, and stable, a firm foundation, and unmoving from your confession of faith. Stay your course by getting God's promises firmly rooted in your heart. Speak what God has promised in His Word. Power up by embracing it with all your heart! Reject and rebuke all attempts of the devil, who is trying to steal and stop your answer from manifesting!

Today and every day, be determined, inflexible, and unmoving from what you believe and confess because *He is faithful*!

Prayer:

Lord, there are times when I find it hard to hold onto your promises, especially in the middle of all the chaos in our world and in my life at times. I ask you to give me a steadfast spirit, a heart that follows hard after you and holds to the confidence I have in your Word. I know you are faithful. I know you have the victory and are able and willing to not only care for me in every trial I face but to bring me out on the other side with great victory! In Jesus's name, amen.

Day 32

Overcoming Adversity

"If you faint in the day of adversity, your strength is small."
—Proverbs 24:10

IN THE VERSE ABOVE, *adversity* means distress, tribulations, difficulties, and affliction. And *small* means underdeveloped. Jesus, several times, addressed this concept of "small faith" as little or undeveloped faith.

"And immediately Jesus stretched out His hand and caught him, and said to him, 'O you of little faith, why did you doubt?'"
—Matthew 14:31

This is not condemnation but speaking the Truth in love. How can we develop strength so we do not faint or give up in the time of adversity? Proverbs 24:5 says, *"A wise man is strong, Yes, a man of knowledge increases strength."* People who renew their minds with the Word of God and fill their hearts with the Word of God will increase spiritual strength and faith and will stand strong in the day of adversity.

How much time are you giving to God's Word? When adversity shows up, whatever comes out of your mouth is the condition of your heart. The more time you spend in God's Word, the more your words will reflect His power over your troubles. Power up by reading His Word every day!

"I would have lost heart, unless I had believed that I would see the goodness of the Lord in the land of the living."
—Psalm 27:13

"And since we have the same spirit of faith, according to what is written, "I believed and therefore I spoke," we also believe and therefore speak."
—2 Corinthians 4:13

Prayer:

Father, you have ordained victory for my life and provide a solution in every trial and with every adversary I face. I know I do not face them alone, for you are with me and will never leave me! I do not want my strength to be small in the day of adversity; therefore, I will make your Word my rock and my dwelling place. I will claim the promise in your Word: *"Remember the word to Your servant, upon which You have caused me to hope. This is my comfort in my affliction, for Your word has given me life."* (Ps. 119:49–50) In Jesus's name, amen.

Day 33

Praise! The Voice of Faith

"Who, contrary to hope, in hope believed, so that he became the father of many nations, according to what was spoken, 'So shall your descendants be.' And not being weak in faith, he did not consider his own body, already dead (since he was about a hundred years old), and the deadness of Sarah's womb. He did not waver at the promise of God through unbelief, but was strengthened in faith, giving GLORY (Praise & Worship) to God, and being fully convinced that what He had promised He was also able to perform."
—Romans 4:18-21

THIS SCRIPTURE SPEAKS OF Abraham and the promise of a son that God had given him, even though it was naturally impossible for this to happen. Abraham believed God and saw the promise manifested.

How do you know you're in faith and truly believing like Abraham? Listen to the words coming out of your mouth concerning your situation. Are you praising God because you are fully convinced that what He promised is yours? Or are you praising just because somebody preached it? Praise is an outward expression of our inner faith and the fervent passion that arises from our hearts of faith. Praise connects with our mouths and declares, "God promised it, I believe it, and that settles it, so hear me roar through my praise that I have what He has promised!"

Fear will flee, anxiety will vanish, and faith in God will ascend and dominate your emotions and feelings because your praise focus is on our Heavenly Father! Praise Him because of what He has said. Power up by letting your praise drown out the voice of your circumstance. When He inhabits your praise, the enemy exits. Get your praise on!

> ### Prayer:
> Father, my heart desires to be like Abraham. I believe; please conquer my unbelief that creeps in at times. Forgive me for the times when I have not believed or when I faltered when I thought the promise was taking too long. Continue to uphold me in my time of trial, and increase my faith to walk boldly without wavering, no matter what I see, knowing assuredly that I will see what you have promised me. In the time of waiting, I will give you praise and worship for who you are, for your faithfulness to your Word and to me! In Jesus's name, amen.

Praise is an outward expression of our inner faith.

Day 34

Greater Is He Who Is in You

"You are of God, little children, and have overcome them,
because He who is in you is greater than he who is in the world."
—1 John 4:4

AS WE WALK IN difficult seasons in our nation and the world, decide that you are not going to allow anything or anyone to intimidate you. Remember, you are plugged into the most powerful source in the universe—God Himself lives in you. You have the right and privilege to pray, and you have the authority to use the name of Jesus. You have God's promises, and He stands behind every word! This doesn't mean that everything will manifest overnight, but you're guaranteed that things will turn and change for your good.

Romans 8:27–28 promises this: *"Now He who searches the hearts knows what the mind of the Spirit is, because He makes intercession for the saints according to the will of God. And we know that all things work together for good to those who love God, to those who are the called according to His purpose."*

"Not a word failed of any good thing which the LORD *had spoken*

to the house of Israel. All came to pass."
—Joshua 21:45

This is our God! Walk with confidence like Jesus, knowing that His Father loved Him unconditionally. But do not be ego-driven; be Kingdom-driven by love. Don't be rude or judgmental, but walk in love, and be an encourager. Lift people up; don't tear them down. Make a difference. Be the Light everywhere you go, and do not be intimidated by the darkness. Power up!

Prayer:

Father, you have been faithful to keep me in every situation and the obstacles that come into my life to derail me. You are walking with me in this season, no matter what the future holds. I know your Word tells me that you have good plans for me! I will not allow intimidation to rule me. I will stand in the Truth that you are bigger in me than anything I will ever face. I pray that love, peace, and joy will rule my heart and that it spill over onto every person I meet! In Jesus's name, amen.

Day 35

What to Do When You Want to Give Up and Give In

"Because your words are my deepest delight, I didn't give up when all else was lost.
I can never forget the profound revelations you've taught me,
for they have kept me alive more than once."
—Psalm 119:92–93 (TPT)

PROVERBS 4:21-22 (TPT) TELLS us to attend to God's Word: *"Fill your thoughts with my words until they penetrate deep into your spirit. Then, as you unwrap my words, they will impart true life and radiant health into the very core of your being."*

Why is this so important? Because the enemy will put thoughts in your mind that are contrary to God's Word. He knows that the more you fill your mind and heart with God's Word, the more you will declare His promises and that God will fulfill His Word. The enemy immediately tries to steal God's Word by attacking your mind with negative statements. According to Mark 4:14–15, *"The sower sows the word. And these are the ones by the wayside where the word is sown. When they hear, Satan comes immediately and takes away (make to doubt) the word that was sown in their hearts."* Rebuke every thought that is contrary to God's Word!

The enemy will turn up the heat and send those negative words our way like *fiery darts*, which the Word calls them in James. Power up by taking the sword of the Spirit and cutting those negative words to pieces. Keep the shield of faith, and keep declaring and believing God's Word.

Keep going!

Prayer:

Lord, there are times in this fight when I've grown weary—so weary that I wanted to give up. I thank you, God, that it's not by my might that I stand, but by your Holy Spirit. Lord, continue to teach and instruct me in your Word so I will have the strength to stand. I know I have the victory in this situation, no matter what I see. Encourage and comfort me by your Holy Spirit in me! In Jesus's name, amen.

Day 36

Are You Passing the Test?

"Until the time that his word came to pass, the word of the LORD tested him."
—Psalm 105:19

THIS SCRIPTURE SPEAKS OF the life of Joseph during an unpleasant time he experienced. God had shown him a dream, but the dream did not come to pass overnight. Joseph went through some extremely difficult times, and during those times, he was severely tested regarding whether or not he would stay committed to the Word of God.

He faced betrayal, temptation, disappointment, loneliness, false accusations, and discouragement. He could have easily given up. I'm sure the devil was attacking his mind with statements like, "You'll never see your dream come true. God was lying to you. If He really loved you, then this wouldn't be happening to you." Sound familiar? The devil does the same thing to us, but he is a liar! Joseph was being tested by the Word of God. Would he give in to his trials and temptations to quit, or would he keep believing, enduring, and persevering? His final deliverance did not happen overnight, but eventually, God turned his ashes into success and his mourning into joy.

We are facing difficult times. Will we throw in the towel and quit believing, praying, and praising? Or will we throw down on the devil the difficulties and circumstances and keep advancing and growing spiritually?

Joseph kept on believing, and we saw his outcome! This is just a test, but we are going to pass it, and we will see deliverance and victory. Keep on keeping on. Power up by continuing to believe, endure, and persevere!

Prayer:

Father, these days that are upon us have become a trial and test to me. There are days when the pressures overwhelm me. Help me keep my heart and my trust in your Word, no matter what I see or experience. Although it may be hard, like it was for Joseph, I know this is only a test, and I will pass it in Jesus's name. I will be able to endure and emerge at the end fulfilling the Word you have spoken over my life, just as Joseph did. In Jesus's name, amen.

Day 37

Your Image of Yourself Determines Your Victory

"There we saw the giants (the descendants of Anak came from the giants); and we were like grasshoppers in our own sight, and so we were in their sight."
—Numbers 13:33

OUR BEHAVIOR IS DETERMINED by what's in our heart. There is a King inside each of us, so why do we allow insecurities to dominate our actions? Do you see yourself as God sees you? Greater is He who is in you than he that is in the world! Greatness is in you! How you see yourself will determine what you believe you can accomplish. How you see yourself will determine your next move—to advance in faith or to retreat in fear.

The way you see yourself will carry you to the heights of success or into the depths of despair and defeat. A distorted image will cripple you for life! Be who God says you are, not who others want you to be or you used to be. You are a new creation! See yourself as more than a conqueror. With God on your side, you can't be defeated unless you see yourself as less than how God sees you.

The test of courage comes when you stand for what God says, live according to His standards, and walk with no compromise when you are in the minority. You can only conquer what you are willing to confront! The Lion of Judah lives in you. You're not a fraidy-cat. Power up by letting the lion in you roar! Be who God declares you are—today and forever!

"Be strong and of good courage, do not fear nor be afraid of them;
for the LORD your God, He is the One who goes with you.
He will not leave you nor forsake you."
—Deuteronomy 31:6

Prayer:

Father, I have allowed the past to define how I see myself! I have allowed the enemy to heap condemnation and fear upon my image of myself and have lived in defeat! But I take upon me, the image of who you have made me, in Christ! A new creation, your workmanship (Eph. 2:10, NKJV) created in Christ Jesus! Created in the image of God for good works! Help me to renew my mind in your Word and be transformed by the renewing of my mind to see myself like you do! I love you, Lord! In Jesus's name, amen.

The way you see yourself will carry you either to the heights of success or into the depths of despair and defeat.

Day 38

Fear Not!

"For God has not given us a spirit of fear, but of power and of love and of a sound mind."
—2 Timothy 1:7

FEAR WANTS YOU TO run from something that isn't after you. A great evangelist once said, "Fear knocked at my door. Faith answered... and there was no one there." That's the proper response to fear. The worst we can imagine almost never happens, and most worries die in vain anticipation.

Fear holds you back from flexing your faith muscle. It's been said that worry is a darkroom where negatives are developed. Fear and worry are like a rocking chair; they keep you moving in the wrong mindset, and you don't get anywhere. Most of our fears can be traced back to a fear of man. But the Bible says in Psalm 27:1, *"The LORD is the strength of my life; of whom then shall I be afraid?"* People would worry less about what others think of them if they only realized how seldom they do. They are probably wondering what you're thinking of them!

Many people are so filled with fear that they go through life never attempting anything in faith; and therefore never experience the joy of accomplishing their God-designed assignments. Fear of the future is a waste of the present. Fear not tomorrow, for God has already been there and has great things planned for you! Yes, there will be difficulties and hindrances, but that is why you develop your faith. Do not feed your fears. Instead, power up by starving them to death!

"For I know the thoughts that I think toward you, says the LORD, thoughts of peace and not of evil, to give you a future and a hope."
—Jeremiah 29:11

Prayer:

Father, I know you have not given me the spirit of fear. There are times when my mind is drawn away to a place of fear and my thoughts get away from me to a place of dread. Lord, help me keep my mind focused on you and your Word. I pray for your peace to be released in my situation now, in Jesus's name, and I thank you for that peace. In Jesus's name, amen.

Day 39

Who Is Stronger?

"Let me illustrate this further. Who is powerful enough to enter the house of a strong man like Satan and plunder his goods? Only someone even stronger—someone who could tie him up and then plunder his house."
—Mark 3:27 (NLT)

REMEMBER, WE ARE THE stronger ones. We have been given all power over Satan and the kingdom of darkness. It says in 1 John 4:4, *"You are of God, little children, and have overcome them, because He who is in you is greater than he who is in the world."*

As the Church, we can plunder the kingdom of darkness in every city through intercessory prayer, pulling down the strongholds, healing the sick, and loosing the captives to be born again! Are you using the keys that He's given us? Every believer has the keys, and no one is left out—but are you using them? You can't complain and feel sorry for yourself if you're not using the tools that Jesus has given you.

"And I will give you the keys of the kingdom of heaven, and whatever you bind on earth will be bound in heaven, and whatever

you loose on earth will be loosed in heaven."
—Matthew 16:19

It's time to rally the troops and get back to activating the keys and serious intercession. Power up by using the keys He has given you!

"Ask me to give you the nations (the lost) and I will do it,
And they shall become your legacy.
Your domain will stretch to the ends of the earth.
And you will rule over them with unlimited authority,
Crushing their rebellion as
An iron rod smashes jars of clay!"
—Psalm 2:8–9 (TPT)

> ### *Prayer:*
> Father God, I thank you that you have given me the keys to the Kingdom. Thank you for the power of the Holy Spirit to break every bond of the enemy. Lord, stir my heart again for intercession and ignite compassion into my heart for the lost. The same heart that Jesus had to restore the lost, let that heart be in me and help me to be faithful to your call to intercession in Jesus's name, amen.

We have been given all power over Satan and the kingdom of darkness.

Day 40

He's Still the All-Sufficient God

"I have been young, and now am old; yet I have not seen the righteous forsaken, nor his descendants begging bread."
—Psalm 37:25

HE IS STILL THE God of the impossible! He fed all the children of Israel when they went into the wilderness, and He can still take care of His kids! But we must ask Him in faith, based on His promises. Matthew 7:11 (NKJV) says, *"If you then, being evil, know how to give good gifts to your children, how much more will your Father who is in heaven give good things to those who ask Him!"*

He will not leave you or forsake you. He can prepare a table for you in the presence of your enemies. He is El Shaddai, *the all-powerful and all-sufficient God*, the God who is *more than enough!* He is Jehovah Jireh, the Lord who *sees and provides*. But we must ask Him and be specific concerning our needs.

"Ask, and it will be given to you; seek, and you will find; knock, and it will be opened to you. For everyone who asks receives, and

he who seeks finds, and to him who knocks it will be opened."
—Luke 11:9–13

Power up by asking Him for what you need in faith, based on His promises!

> **Prayer:**
> Father, thank you for never leaving me or forsaking me. Thank you for your faithfulness to always provide for me. I come asking, seeking, and knocking today for you to provide all my needs. *(Tell Him what those needs are.)* It may seem to us like lack is taking over the situation, but you have never forsaken those who trust in you. I lay all my needs at your feet and trust that you will meet all of them. In Jesus's name, amen.

He can prepare a table for you in the presence of your enemies.

Day 41

Words on Assignment

"Then God said, 'Let there be light'; and there was light."
—Genesis 1:3

OVER AND OVER, WE read, "And God said, 'Let there be...'" The words that spoke out of His mouth were sent on assignment to bring forth what He believed in His heart. Are your words on assignment? What words are you assigning to your situation? If you're assigning His Words to your situation, then you can expect powerful results!

Isaiah 55:11 (MSG) states, *"My words will accomplish the assignment I gave them."* When He speaks something into the Earth, He says, "My words have assignments on them. They will accomplish what I have assigned them to do." Be diligent about the words you're speaking. Are you speaking His words?

"You will also declare a thing, and it will be established
for you; So light will shine on your ways."
—Job 22:28

There should not be a day that goes by that you are not declaring and decreeing something into the atmosphere over your situations, your life, and your family according to God's Word.

No word spoken by God, that is now spoken through you, will return to Him without having accomplished something on the Earth. Power up by putting your words on assignment—not just for yourself, but for others also.

Prayer:

Holy Father, your words are alive and powerful! Thank you for your Word that you've given to me. It is full of promises and wisdom for every situation that I face. Today, I speak your Word over the circumstances of my life in the following areas (*list or say what those areas are*). As you promised, that Word will not return void but will accomplish everything intended for me from your Word and your will. In Jesus's name, amen.

No word, spoken by God through you, will return to Him without having accomplished something on the earth.

Day 42

✳ Be Anxious for Nothing ✳

"Therefore, do not worry about tomorrow, for tomorrow will worry about its own things. Sufficient for the day is its own trouble."
—Matthew 6:34

JESUS TOLD US NOT to worry. Why would He make such a statement? Is it that He's gone back to heaven and doesn't understand that we're still on this earth dealing with all this mess, trying to make it and figure out how we're going to pay these bills? Not at all. Read Matthew 6:25–34 again, and take your time. Verse 32 states, *"Therefore, indeed, seeing that, your Heavenly Father knows that you need all these things."*

You might say, "That's great, but I need Him to do something!" Well, He needs *you* to do something. Focus on verse 33: *"…but seek first the Kingdom of God."* In Greek, the word "but" is *de* and is the root word of *deesis*, which means prayer, petition, and supplication. He knows, He sees, and He's ready and willing! Are you asking or worrying? Fear and worry will negate your prayers if you speak in agreement with them after you have prayed. This is the way the Kingdom of God operates. Rebuke fear and anxiety. Ask, and keep on asking in faith.

Have you forgotten 1 John 5:14–15? He knows, He cares, and He moves when you ask in accordance with His Word. Are you just crying out in generalities, or are you asking for what you need specifically? Ask, and you shall receive. Power up by trusting Him in faith, doubting nothing! Feed your faith, and choke out your doubts. God doesn't move because of your *feelings*; He moves because of your *faith*.

Prayer:

Father, thank you for the amazing way you care for me. The fact that you know what I need brings me great comfort. But there are times when I become overwhelmed with my needs and allow worry to flood my heart. Lord, help me keep my eyes and my heart on your Kingdom and your righteousness and not be concerned for my needs. Help me understand how important it is to seek your Kingdom first, above all things. In Jesus's name, amen.

Day 43

Prayer Is the Principal Thing

"Then He came to the disciples and found them sleeping, and said to Peter, 'What! Could you not watch with Me one hour? Watch and pray, lest you enter into temptation. The spirit indeed is willing, but the flesh is weak.'"
—Matthew 26:40-41

WHAT DOES JESUS FIND when He comes to us or to His church? Does He find us spiritually sleeping? What was a major concentration of His life? Hebrews 5:7 reveals, *"Who, in the days of His flesh, when He had offered up prayers and supplications, with vehement cries and tears to Him who was able to save Him from death, and was heard because of His godly fear."*

We are living in the last days, and we are experiencing intense spiritual warfare. Your success will be determined by your prayer life and the depth of God's Word in your heart. Peter slept instead of praying. He fell into temptation just a few hours later. Delilah lulled Samson to sleep; she couldn't do anything while he was awake and strong! Martha was too busy to spend time at the feet of Jesus like Mary; therefore, Martha's life was full of worry and anxiety.

How is your life today? Check your prayer life. That is where you will find your solutions, guidance, and answers. Mark 9:29 says, *"So He said to them, 'This kind can come out by nothing but prayer and fasting.'"* This is one of the keys to the impossible.

Power up by fortifying yourself with prayer and the depth of God's Word in your heart!

Prayer:

Father, my prayer life often does not measure up to that modeled in the Bible. I am often like Peter and Martha instead of Mary, and I recognize how that affects my life. My desire is to live a life of prayer, not only when I need something, but to express thanksgiving and worship. I desire a life of prayer in the Spirit to guide me when I don't know how to pray. Thank you, Lord, for continuing to teach me to pray as Jesus taught His disciples. In Jesus's name, amen.

Day 44

The Word of His Power

"For as the rain comes down, and the snow from heaven, and do not return there, but water the earth, and make it bring forth and bud, that it may give seed to the sower and bread to the eater, So shall My word be that goes forth from My mouth; It shall not return to Me void, but it shall accomplish what I please, and it shall prosper in the thing for which I sent it."
—Isaiah 55:10

WHEN YOU SPEAK WHAT God speaks, His Word always prevails in every situation. Nothing is impossible with God, and nothing is beyond His power. We release that power when we believe and speak His Word! When we believe and speak His Word, all the forces of nature, every demon, and even the angels of heaven must obey because God's Word is the final authority in all matters and in every situation.

Hebrews 1:3 tells us that He is upholding all things by word of His power. Are the words that are coming out of your mouth upholding or tearing down? You're either releasing heaven to work on your behalf, or you're releasing hell—it's your choice. God fulfills His Word, and the devil will fulfill his words coming out of a negative mouth. Power up by speaking God's Word! It is seed and will bring an abundant harvest.

> *"Wise words satisfy like a good meal;*
> *The right words bring satisfaction.*
> *The tongue can bring death or life;*
> *Those who love to talk will reap the consequences."*
> —Proverbs 18:20-21 (NLT)

Prayer:

Father, forgive me for allowing negative words to come out of my mouth. Forgive me for agreeing with the devil and for failing to take hold of your Word in my situations. Thank you for forgiving me, helping me, and reminding me, by your Holy Spirit, to always choose your Word as my declaration! In Jesus's name, amen.

Nothing is impossible with God or beyond His power!

Day 45

Change Your Focus

"There we saw the giants (the descendants of Anak came from the giants); and we were like grasshoppers in our own sight, and so we were in their sight."
—Numbers 13:33

YOUR FUTURE IS NOT determined by where you were born or came from, the family you came from, what vocation you're in, or what has happened to you. Instead, it's determined by how you see yourself and how you perceive your circumstances. Proverbs 23:7 says, *"For as he thinks in his heart, so is he."* How you see yourself and what you believe can carry you to the heights of success and blessings, or it can plunge you into the depths of despair, ruin, and defeat.

It's not the things that happen to you in life that cause you to fail or succeed; it's the way you see things, what you believe and pray about the things you see, and what you speak about the things you see after you pray. Whatever is in your heart when you see things—whatever you believe about what you see—will come out of your mouth in the form of either faith or unbelief. What you speak is what you believe will happen, and what you believe and speak will manifest.

*"And since we have the same spirit of faith, according to
what is written, 'I believed and therefore I spoke,'
we also believe and therefore speak."*
—2 Corinthians 4:13

If you want to have success, first look into God's Word, see His Promises, and see your situation from His perspective, which should be your perspective. Then move forward and address your situation according to, and in agreement with, His Word. Then, with praise and thanksgiving, receive what He has promised. If you constantly complain, you will remain in discomfort, but if you Praise, you will be raised into victory! Changing your focus will change the way you pray and speak.

Power up by seeing yourself the way He sees you!

Prayer:

Dear Father, thank you for encouraging me to get my eyes off the issues of my life and get them on your might and power over me. You are the Almighty God, and my problems don't stand a chance facing you. Therefore, I will put my eyes on you and my trust in your Word and your love. Forgive me for any words I've spoken to the contrary. In Jesus's name, amen.

Day 46

Never Alone

"Indeed, the hour is coming, yes, has now come, that you will be scattered, each to his own, and will leave Me alone. And yet I am not alone, because the Father is with Me."
—John 16:32

THERE ARE TIMES IN our lives when we feel all alone and we can't feel God's presence. We ask, "Where are you, Lord?" Jesus lived by a statement His Heavenly Father made to Him: no matter how difficult things got, He pressed on because He knew in His heart that He was loved unconditionally and never forsaken!

"And suddenly a voice came from heaven, saying, 'This is My beloved Son, in whom I am well pleased.'"
—Matthew 3:17

You are God's beloved, too, and you always will be! You might feel lonely, but you're never alone. When you ask, "God where are you?" listen to His response. Hebrews 13:5–6 (AMP) says, *"For He has said, 'I will never [under any circumstances] desert you [nor give you up nor leave you without support, nor will I in any degree leave you helpless], nor will I for-*

sake or let you down or relax My hold on you [assuredly not]!' So we take comfort and are encouraged and confidently say, 'THE LORD IS MY HELPER [in time of need], I WILL NOT BE AFRAID. WHAT WILL MAN DO TO ME'?"

Power up, and claim His promise that He will never desert you!

Prayer:

Father, I take great comfort and strength in knowing that even when I feel alone, your Word assures me that you are ever-present. You will never leave me. Because of this promise, I am confident and can say with assurance that I will not be afraid. Lord, at times it's hard to remember this when all hell is breaking loose in my life. But I will trust that in whatever circumstance I face, I'm not in it by myself. You are there. And if you're there, that's all I need to know. Thank you, Father! In Jesus's name, amen.

You may have feelings of loneliness, but you are never alone!

Day 47

Your Position vs. Your Condition

"...And raised us up together and made us sit together in the heavenly places in Christ Jesus."
—Ephesians 2:6

MANY CHRISTIANS FOCUS MORE on their current condition than on their current position, based on their eternal life in Christ Jesus. Any *condition* is temporary and subject to change, but our *position* in Christ is eternal. The Scripture in 2 Corinthians 4:18 confirms this: *"...while we do not look at the things which are seen, but at the things which are not seen. For the things which are seen are temporary, but the things which are not seen are eternal."*

Don't ignore your current condition, but pray and address it in accordance with your position in Jesus and according to His Word. How do you do that?

Mark 11:23–24 tells us, *"For assuredly, I say to you, whoever says to this mountain, 'Be removed and be cast into the sea,' and does not doubt in his heart, but believes that those things he says will be done, he will have whatever he says. Therefore I say to you, whatever things you ask when you pray, believe that you receive them, and you will have them."*

Power up by focusing on your eternal position in Christ!

Prayer:

Father, thank you that you have placed me in a heavenly place eternally. Sometimes that Truth slips out of my vision when my condition or problem is staring me in the face. Help me to live convinced that eternal things are stronger and surer than the temporal conditions of my life. Thank you for always being merciful and patient with me as I embrace this Truth and walk it out in my life. In Jesus's name, amen.

Any condition is temporary and subject to change, but our position in Christ is eternal.

Day 48

Keep Your Eyes on the Road

"Brethren, I do not count myself to have apprehended; but one thing I do, forgetting those things which are behind and reaching forward to those things which are ahead, I press toward the goal for the prize of the upward call of God in Christ Jesus."
—Philippians 3:13-14

REMEMBER WHEN MY driver's ed teacher told me I should use my rearview mirror for perspective, but not to fixate on it. He said if I spent too much of my time looking backward, then I was guaranteed to have an accident.

Great wisdom for our lives is that if we keep looking into the past, we can be sure that we'll end up wrecking our future. When you're driving, you're concentrating on what's in front of you because that's where you're going. To reach God's destination successfully, you must keep your eyes on His Word. Psalm 119:105 says, *"Your word is a lamp to my feet and a light to my path."*

The Apostle Paul had a terrible past, but as he stated in the Scripture above, he was forgetting those things so he could move forward. It's time for you to move forward, press on, and live your life looking forward by looking at all the promises God has given you! Power up by rebuking the thoughts that come into your mind about your past! Keep moving forward into your God-ordained future.

"Study this Book of Instruction continually. Meditate on it day and night so you will be sure to obey everything written in it. Only then will you prosper and succeed in all you do. This is my command—be strong and courageous! Do not be afraid or discouraged. For the LORD your God is with you wherever you go."
—Joshua 1:8–9 (NLT)

Prayer:

Father, thank you for the vision you have for my life. At times I get stuck in my past, and it's hard to move beyond it. But you've shown me in your Word that those things are forgiven and over. Your Word tells me through Paul to forget the things behind and move forward. I ask you to help me do that. I lay my past at your feet and ask you to give me the power to release it and go forward into your great plan for me. In Jesus's name, amen.

Day 49

Unlimited Potential/ Infinite Possibility

"So God created man in His own image; in the image of God He created him; male and female He created them. Then God blessed them, and God said to them, 'Be fruitful and multiply; fill the earth and subdue it; have dominion over the fish of the sea, over the birds of the air, and over every living thing that moves on the earth.'"
—Genesis 1:27-28

YOUR POTENTIAL IS THE power of the Holy Spirit inside you. You have unlimited possibilities! Don't just imagine who you can be because of Christ; realize who you already are in His image, overflowing with His life and power! You have a supernatural bank of resources and latent abilities within you! Yet in many cases, that potential remains untapped and waiting to be discovered to become all kinds of possibilities!

His power can lead you to be all He created you to be. He has given you the power to achieve, power to fulfill His destiny for you and for others whom you will touch and influence. You have a preordained destiny and unlimited potential, and He has chosen you to express a meaning of His life to all you come in contact with: family, friends, coworkers, people in the marketplace, fellow churchgoers—the people you interact with wherever you go. Go with confidence because God has already pre-ordained your journey.

Power up! It's time to get out of the boat and walk on the water of your true potential.

He's calling you to step out of the old and into the new—to step out in faith.

> *"And Peter answered Him and said, 'Lord, if it is You,*
> *command me to come to You on the water.' So, He said, 'Come.'*
> *And when Peter had come down out of the boat,*
> *he walked on the water to go to Jesus."*
> —Matthew 14:28-29

> *"I can do all things through Christ who strengthens me."*
> —Philippians 4:13

Prayer:

I recognize that my potential is limitless because of the Holy Spirit in me. What a huge thought, but it's one I can realize because of the Power in me! Oh Lord, how I long to walk in that potential but fall so short because of my limited thinking. You created in me the mind of Christ, so help me realize my potential and walk in it. Help me see with your eyes, hear with your ears, and live my life according to your will in every moment and every situation. No more small or limited thinking—I can do *all things* through Christ! *Always!* Thank you, Lord. In Jesus's name, amen.

It's time to get out of the boat and walk on the waters of your true potential.

Day 50

Believe What God Says about You

"For the weapons of our warfare are not carnal but mighty in God for pulling down strongholds, casting down arguments and every high thing that exalts itself against the knowledge of God, bringing every thought into captivity to the obedience of Christ."
—2 Corinthians 10:4–5

YOU ARE NOT DEFEATED by the words or sentences that people hurl at you like rocks, even though words are very hurtful. You're defeated only when you believe those nasty words and act as if they're true. You must realize that the devil can use people to speak lies to you to keep you in bondage by believing those lies. Death and life are in the power of the tongue. Start speaking life to yourself; speak what God says about you. Don't believe what others have said; believe the Word of God. Cast down every word and thought contrary to what God says about you. Stop listening to lies that promote failure. Power up, and start declaring Truth!

You are the beloved of God, the righteousness of God in Christ Jesus, loved unconditionally by God. You are His precious treasure, the apple of His eye, valuable and invaluable, one of a kind, appreciated and admired, held dear in His heart, prized above all other things, favored and preferred, chosen and adopted by God, singled out and selected to be His own, well liked, and blessed!

Today, *"put off the old man and put on the new man which was created according to God, in true righteousness and holiness and be renewed in the spirit of your mind"* (Eph. 4:22–24).

> *"For the Lord GOD will help Me;*
> *Therefore I will not be disgraced;*
> *Therefore I have set My face like a flint,*
> *And I know that I will not be ashamed."*
> —Isaiah 50:7

Prayer:

Thank you, Father, for declaring me precious to you! I have let the words of others determine my value and even to determine how you think of me. Forgive me. I set my face like a flint to see and understand only what you say about me and to apply that to everything I think about myself. I pray to be defined only by your love and your Word. Give no other words the power to define me—only your Word! In Jesus's name, amen.

It's not the things that happen to you in life that cause you to fail or succeed, but what you **believe** *about the things that happen to you.*

Day 51

Time to Arise!

"Arise [from the depression and prostration in which circumstances have kept you—
rise to a new life]! Shine (be radiant with the glory of the Lᴏʀᴅ), for your light has
come, and the glory of the Lᴏʀᴅ has risen upon you! For behold, darkness shall cover
the earth, and dense darkness [all] peoples, but the Lᴏʀᴅ shall arise upon you [O
Jerusalem], and His glory shall be seen on you. And nations shall come to your light,
and kings to the brightness of your rising."
—Isaiah 60:1–3 (AMP)

THIS IS A TIME, in history, to get our eyes off ourselves, worldly distractions, and what the darkness is declaring. We must get back to the Commission given to us by the Commander of the Armies of God. Darkness can increase, but it cannot win, defeat, or stop the Light! Darkness wins only when the light is hidden or turned off. Power up by letting Jesus's light shine through you!

"And He said to them, 'Go into all the world and preach the gospel
to every creature. He who believes and is baptized will be saved;
but he who does not believe will be condemned. And these signs
will follow those who believe: In My name they will cast out

demons; they will speak with new tongues; they will take up serpents; and if they drink anything deadly, it will by no means hurt them; they will lay hands on the sick, and they will recover."
—Mark 16:15-18

This will be a time of demonstration and manifestation of the power of the Light. You are the light of the world—don't hold back or obscure the Light!

"Do all things without complaining and disputing, that you may become blameless and harmless, children of God without fault in the midst of a crooked and perverse generation, among whom you shine as lights in the world."
—Philippians 2:14-15

Prayer:

Father, I arise—out of depression. Out of sadness. I arise and set my eyes on Jesus, the Author and Finisher of my faith. I arise to go into the harvest fields of this world. For the harvest is truly great! I pray that you would keep me ever-mindful of those who walk in darkness and who have no hope. Keep my eyes on those who need you. Help me learn to cast my cares on you and not to be so overwhelmed with my own needs that I forget my true calling: to be a minister of reconciliation. In Jesus's name, amen.

Day 52

Truth

"For the word of the LORD is right, and all His work is done in truth."
—Psalm 33:4

THE SPIRIT OF GOD can only work in Truth. If we are not walking in Truth, then He doesn't work in our lives, except for bringing conviction so He can bring us back into Truth. To walk in Truth, live in Truth, and speak Truth means to be led by the Spirit of Truth (John 16:13) and to obey God's Word.

If I depend on lies to help myself, then God is not helping me, and the devil will eventually bring chaos and ruin to my life. The devil is the father of all lies. There is no Truth in him. If you walk, live, and speak Truth, victory is always yours—you can't lose! It may not look or feel like victory, but it will be there because it is yours through Jesus and the Word of God.

"But thanks be to God, who gives us the victory
through our Lord Jesus Christ."
—1 Corinthians 15:57

The Truth will not only *set* you free; it will *keep* you free! No matter what is true about your situation, Truth can overcome what is true. If I'm dealing with sickness, I don't deny it; it is true. But the Truth that His Word declares in 1 Peter 2:24 trumps what may be true in my body. And it's that Truth that I declare over my situation: *"Who Himself bore our sins in His own body on the tree, that we, having died to sins, might live for righteousness—by whose stripes you were healed."*

The Truth is the power of God to set you free! God's promises are His words of Truth to you for every situation of your life. Power up by walking, living, and speaking God's Truth!

> ### *Prayer:*
> Lord, at times it's hard to see the Truth in the midst of what's true in my life. Forgive me for the times when I've accepted a lie above the Truth of your Word in my life. Help me to trust *the* Truth over what may be true in my circumstances. Strengthen me to stand strong on your Truth against every lie of the enemy. In Jesus's name, amen.

The Truth will not only set you free; it will keep you free!

Day 53

Unshakable Faith

*"I stand silently to listen for the one I love, waiting as long as it takes
for the Lord to rescue me.*

*For God alone has become my Savior. He alone is my safe place; his wrap-around
presence always protects me. For he is my champion defender;
there's no risk of failure with God. So why would I let worry paralyze me,
even when troubles multiply around me?"*
—Psalm 62:1-2 (TPT)

IF FEAR AND ANXIETY are moving you, then you're believing your doubts about your situation instead of totally trusting God and His Word. Cast out those negative thoughts, and declare God's Word to your situation! Declare the Scripture above to your situation. Your God is your champion defender. He cannot fail. When you declare the Truth of God, faith begins to rise up in you. Declaring Truth puts the spotlight on God and His power.

Hebrews 6:12 tells us that through faith and patience, we inherit the promises of God. *Patience* means how I behave and how I speak until I see my prayer answered. I'm moved by what God says—His promises—not by what I see, hear, or feel in the natural realm. Faith moves you toward God, while fear and anxiety move you in the wrong direction.

So let the Holy Spirit's GPS reroute you back in the right direction of what God says, not what you feel or how your emotions are causing you to react. The Holy Spirit will always reroute you back to the Truth of His Word. Power up, and declare the Truth of God!

Prayer:

Father, I thank you for your Word and for your promises that are all *yes*! Thank you for building patience in me as I wait with expectancy for the answer to my prayers. Thank you for your faithfulness over my life and for Jesus, who is the Author and Finisher of my faith. Hallelujah! In Jesus's name, amen.

Day 54

What Are Your Words Producing?

"Who have said, 'With our tongue we will prevail;
our lips are our own; Who is lord over us?'"
—Psalm 12:4

WORDS ARE ONE OF the most powerful forces in the universe. God created this world with the power of His words. Even those who are not Christians believe in the power of their words. Even the devil knows the power of words and confessing words!

"For you have said in your heart: 'I will ascend into heaven,
I will exalt my throne above the stars of God; I will also sit on the
mount of the congregation on the farthest sides of the north;
I will ascend above the heights of the clouds,
I will be like the Most High.'"
—Isaiah 14:13–14

The devil's words had no power over God, but God's Word has all power over the devil, demons, and circumstances that are contrary to God's will. What is coming out of your mouth concerning your situation? Why should you speak God's Word continually until you see things turn for your favor? Jeremiah 1:12 (AMP) tells us, *"Then the* Lord *said to me, 'You have seen well, for I am [actively] watching over My word to fulfill it.'"*

Your words are either empowering the kingdom of darkness or the Kingdom of God. Which result do you want? Power up, and use your words to exalt Him!

> *"I call heaven and earth as witnesses today against you, that I have set before you life and death, blessing and cursing; therefore choose life, that both you and your descendants may live."*
> —Deuteronomy 30:19

Prayer:

Lord, help me speak what you speak and declare what you declare. Help me always be mindful of what is coming out of my mouth. I don't want to empower the kingdom of darkness with my words. Help me faithfully declare the Word of your Kingdom, Lord! In Jesus's name, amen.

Words are the most powerful force in the universe.

Day 55

Spiritual Warfare, A Present-Day Reality

"Finally, my brethren, be strong in the Lord and in the power of His might. Put on the whole armor of God, that you may be able to stand against the wiles of the devil. For we do not wrestle against flesh and blood, but against principalities, against powers, against the rulers of the darkness of this age, against spiritual hosts of wickedness in the heavenly places. Therefore, take up the whole armor of God, that you may be able to withstand in the evil day, and having done all, to stand."
—Ephesians 6:10-13

T SHOCKS ME TO see little or no emphasis on the root cause of all the evil and wickedness we see in our nation. It's as if spiritual demonic forces are not even mentioned in church dialogue anymore. The concentration seems to be more on natural thinking, cultural wisdom, or psychological reasoning for the tragic events happening on a regular basis. The church is the only ordained institution, by Jesus, to have power over, and to deal with, these demonic forces. Jesus spent much of His ministry casting out demons. Has this changed or passed away concerning His church? *No!* John 14:12 tells us, *"Most assuredly, I say to you, he who believes in Me, the works that I do he will do also; and greater works than these he will do, because I go to My Father."*

We must get back to spiritual intercession and spiritual warfare for our nation, our cities, and systems so that interference from the kingdom of darkness or the devil will have no influence on them. Where are the prayer warriors who are not afraid of demonic powers and principalities? Where are churches calling people to come to prayer meetings? Are we just too busy with our personal lives or too wrapped up in pleasure to understand the spiritual threat of our day? We must re-examine our priorities and get back to our responsibilities as Christians, or we will lose our freedoms! We must get back to the power of the Holy Spirit, the Word of God, and prayer with boldness.

Power up, and declare spiritual warfare against evil!

"To the intent that now the manifold wisdom of God might be made known by the church to the principalities and powers in the heavenly places."
—Ephesians 3:10

Prayer:
Dear Father, awaken the church. Awaken the sleepers. Lord, strengthen us, your people, to arise to intercession. Open our eyes, and cease our apathy and lethargy so we can see the day we are living in and the necessity of our intercession. Burn your fire in cold hearts to come alive again to you and to pray! Cause us, Lord God, to be watchmen on the wall. In Jesus's name, amen.

Day 56

Keys of the Kingdom

"And I will give you the keys of the kingdom of heaven, and whatever you bind on earth will be bound in heaven, and whatever you loose on earth will be loosed in heaven."
—Matthew 16:19

THE KEYS REPRESENT THE authority of the Kingdom of God that Jesus passed to believers. We have His authority; we don't have to pray for it. He didn't say that we must pray to Him, for He will bind the enemy or loose someone from their chains of sin. No, He said, "*Whatever you bind and loose…*" (Luke 11:21–22).

Mark 3:27 states, "*No one can enter a strong man's house and plunder his goods, unless he first binds the strong man. And then he will plunder his house.*"

When a strong man, fully armed, guards his own palace, his goods are safe. But when a stronger man comes upon him and overcomes him, he takes from him all his armor in which he trusted and divides his spoils.

As a believer, you are the stronger one in Christ! Don't let the devil spoil your house or anyone else's; use your God-delegated authority to bind the powers of darkness, and command them to get out. Set people free from the power of sin, sickness, and poverty by releasing God's

Word and binding the enemy. Don't give him any place in your life or home today—or any day. If you don't use your God-ordained authority, the devil will know it and will constantly steal, kill, and destroy your dreams. Power up! Take and use your God-given authority against the powers of darkness!

Prayer:

Thank you, Father, that you have given me the keys to your Kingdom. You have given me your authority. In Jesus's name I bind every principality operating in my life and family that tries to bring destruction. I rebuke those evil forces and command them by the authority of Jesus's name to loose my family, me, my city, and my nation from (*name those things*). In the name of Jesus, amen.

Day 57

The Power within You

"At my first defense no man stood with me, but all forsook me.
May it not be charged against them."
—2 Timothy 4:16

PAUL DESCRIBES ONE OF his most difficult emotional times in the passage above. Can you imagine that? The great apostle had no one! He felt abandoned and all alone. Have you ever felt like that? Have you ever felt that no one else in the whole world understood you or was willing to stand by you?

It's during those times that we must learn (like Paul) to draw on the strength of Jesus Christ alone. Paul went on to say in 2 Timothy 4:17, *"However, the Lord stood with me and strengthened me, so that the message might be preached fully through me, and that all the Gentiles might hear. And I was delivered out of the mouth of the lion."*

You, too, can learn to draw on the strength of Christ during difficult times. Remember, in every situation you face, it's four against one—the Father, Jesus, the Holy Spirit, and you against your adversary! You're never alone. You might have feelings of loneliness and helplessness, but in reality, you have got the Holy Spirit inside you!

Hebrews 13:5–6 (AMP) says, "...*For He has said, I* will never *[under any circumstances]* desert you *[nor give you up nor leave you without support, nor will I in any degree leave you helpless],* nor will I forsake or let you down or relax My hold on you) *[assuredly not]! So we take comfort* and *are encouraged* and *confidently say,* 'The Lord is my Helper *[in time of need],* I will not be afraid. What will man do to me?'"

Power up and draw on the strength of Jesus Christ!

> **Prayer:**
> Father, thank you for being with me in and through all the storms of my life. Even when I feel abandoned by others, I know you will never abandon me or forsake me. Today, I ask you, Lord, to strengthen me to walk through every valley and hard place I find myself in. Thank you, Lord, that you uphold me with your righteous right hand (Isa. 41:10) and that I'm never alone. In Jesus's name, amen.

In every situation you face, it's four against one: the Father, Jesus, the Holy Spirit, and you against your adversary.

Day 58

A Kingdom Divided

"Every kingdom divided against itself is brought to desolation,
and every city or house divided against itself will not stand."
—Matthew 12:25

RACISM AND PREJUDICE CAUSE divisions, destruction, anger, death, and hatred. They are the devil's weapons to destroy this nation! We are all created in the image of God; no race is superior to another. God created us to love Him and one another. In 1 John 4:20, we are instructed as follows: *"If someone says, 'I love God,' and hates his brother, he is a liar; for he who does not love his brother whom he has seen, how can he love God whom he has not seen?"*

We must pray for revival in our nation. The only answer to all this deception is Jesus Christ and the church getting back to being the church, not an enterprising entity that is lukewarm. Only Jesus can change the hearts of mankind, so we must pray!

The love of God, the pure Word of God, powerful intercessory prayer, and the power of the Holy Spirit must, once again, dominate the church. We cannot allow this division in Christianity. Jesus prayed for unity. John 17:21 tells us, *"That they all may be one, as You, Father, are in Me, and I in You; that they also may be one in Us, that the world may believe that You sent Me."*

We must pray and ask our heavenly Father to send "laborers into the harvest field." Our love for one another will attract the world to hear the Good News of Jesus Christ. Our unity will release the command of the blessing of God (Ps. 133). Power up, and pray for revival!

Let's pray daily, both individually and collectively.

Prayer:

Father, our nation and even the church is so divided right now. We are seeing the result of that division played out in the death and destruction of our citizens. Violence plagues our cities because of injustice, and we are crying out for justice and peace in our nation. I repent of racial hatred, judgment, and injustice. I repent of selfishness, rebellion, and pride. I cry out for your forgiveness and mercy to be poured into our hearts and lives and into our nation. I pray that your righteousness would reign in our nation. Please, Lord, heal our land. I pray this in Jesus's name, amen.

Day 59

Love One Another

"He has shown you, O man, what is good; and what does the L**ORD** *require of you but to do justly, to love mercy and to walk humbly with your God?"*
—Micah 6:8

IN MATTHEW 22:37-40, THE Lord Jesus tells us what the greatest command is: *"Jesus replied: 'Love the* L**ORD** *your God with all your heart and with all your soul and with all your mind.' This is the first and greatest commandment. And the second is like it: 'Love your neighbor as yourself.' All the Law and the Prophets hang on these two commandments.'"*

God tells us to act justly and to love one another as He has loved us. One of the ways to act justly is to speak out against injustices that happen in our nation. When we see injustice happening to our black brothers and sisters and the white community stays virtually silent, that speaks loudly about our negligence in loving and caring for one another. God is always against injustice!

"Righteousness and justice are the foundation of your throne; love and faithfulness go before you."
—Psalm 89:14

We must speak against injustice and cry out for justice for any race that is experiencing oppression. But we must do it out of love, not hatred and violence, or we will defeat ourselves and take God's justice out of His hands and put it in ours for vengeance. If we cry out to our elected officials on behalf of our brothers and sisters, we will be heard. And when we cry out to God, we will be heard—and both will intervene! There is no place for a silent majority, just like there is no such thing as silent prayer. Power up! Let your voice be heard, but let it be out of a heart of love. Why? Because love never fails!

Prayer:

Father, I ask you to continually give me a heart of love for others and a heart of intercession for the injustices in our world. Give me a heart that beats for my neighbor and for those who are abused, marginalized, and treated unjustly. Give me courage to speak out on their behalf—and also to treat them with love, respect, and compassion. Help me love others as you have loved me, Jesus! In your name I pray, amen.

Day 60

When You Are Weak, That's when You're Strong

"But God has chosen the foolish things of the world to put to shame the wise, and God has chosen the weak things of the world to put to shame the things which are mighty."
—1 Corinthians 1:27

PRAISE GOD! HE HAS chosen all of us—not just the most beautiful, most handsome, most intelligent, most gifted, or strongest—to be his children. He did not choose us because of our natural abilities, looks, or strengths. He chose us in spite of all the ways that we negatively see ourselves sometimes. John 15:16 says, *"You did not choose Me, but I chose you and appointed you that you should go and bear fruit, and that your fruit should remain, that whatever you ask the Father in My name He may give you."*

If you see yourself as weak, not so smart, having a wrong background, growing up on the wrong side of the tracks, not fitting in anywhere, rejected, or a failure in the past, or if you don't seem to belong, then you're God's perfect candidate to accomplish great things for Him!

How about Gideon? In Judges 6:15–16, it says, *"So he said to Him, 'O my Lord, how can I save Israel? Indeed, my clan is the weakest in Manasseh, and I am the least in my father's house.' And the Lord said to him, 'Surely I will be with you, and you shall defeat the Midianites as one man.'"* God was not concerned about Gideon's assessment of himself and his biological background.

How about the Apostle Paul, when he saw himself as inadequate to handle a certain situation? In 2 Corinthians 12:9–10 (MSG), we are made a promise: *"And then He told me, 'My grace is enough; it's all you need. My strength comes into its own in your weakness.' Once I heard that, I was glad to let it happen. I quit focusing on the handicap and began appreciating the gift. It was a case of Christ's strength moving in on my weakness. Now I take limitations in stride, and with good cheer, these limitations that cut me down to size—abuse, accidents, opposition, bad breaks. I just let Christ take over! And so, the weaker I get, the stronger I become."*

Your potential is limitless because of the Holy Spirit inside you. This means you are unlimited in what you can achieve and accomplish for the Kingdom of God. Now, power up! Get up and go forward, mighty man or woman of God!

Prayer:

Dear Lord, so often I perceive my weaknesses as something bad, something to condemn myself for. But you said that when I am weak, that is the moment your strength is made perfect. And although I have made strides in this area, I have such a long way to go in accepting my weaknesses, as Paul did. Help me come to the same understanding as he did about his weaknesses and infirmities through the help of the Holy Spirit. Help me to find glory when I am weak, knowing that in your strength, everything is made perfect. Help me, Lord. In Jesus's name, amen.

The weaker I get, the stronger I become.

Day 61

Deceitful Bow

*"Yet they tested and provoked the Most High God, and did not keep
His testimonies, But turned back and acted unfaithfully like their fathers;
They were turned aside like a deceitful bow."*
—Psalm 78:56-57

THE *DECEITFUL BOW* MENTIONED in the Scripture above was a bow that had become weak because it had been exposed to outside elements that compromised its materials. The bow looked normal, but because of the compromise, its strength and ability were in jeopardy. Therefore, in the time of battle, when the archer would shoot his arrows, the bow would twist, and the arrow would go off course, with the possibility of hitting one of the archer's fellow soldiers.

We are like bows in the hands of our God, shooting the arrows of God's deliverance into the enemy's camp. But if we live with compromise, allow this world to influence us to engage in its lifestyle, or be led by the flesh instead of the Holy Spirit, we will be like deceitful bows. Our arrows can end up hurting those we love, and they will have no impact in defeating the plans and schemes of the kingdom of darkness.

Power up by being a strong bow in the hands of our God so that the enemy fears you! No compromise! Be faithful to God and His Word. Psalm 119:3 (NLT) shows us the way to go: *"They do not compromise with evil, and they walk only in His paths."*

This is the path of righteousness.

Prayer:

Heavenly Father, thank you for your Word and the power of your Spirit to perfect everything that concerns me. Thank you that by your strength, I will not compromise or go down a path of deceit. You have given me power over the voice of the enemy, and I will follow your voice to walk in integrity and obedience to you. Forgive me for the times that I've walked in the flesh or the course of this world. I repent and turn in the direction of your commands and statutes. In Jesus's name, amen.

Day 62

The Power of the Holy Spirit Is Essential

"And suddenly there came a sound from heaven, as of a rushing mighty wind, and it filled the whole house where they were sitting. Then there appeared to them divided tongues, as of fire, and one sat upon each of them. And they were all filled with the Holy Spirit."
—Acts 2:2–4

ONE THING HAS ALWAYS amazed me: the disciples did not weep when Christ left them. They never showed any nostalgia for "the good old days." Luke tells us that after He ascended out of sight, they *"returned to Jerusalem with great joy, and were continually in the temple praising and blessing God"* (Luke 24:52–53). Why did they display such a remarkable reaction to the departure of Jesus? The answer is the coming of the Spirit!

When Christ was present, the disciples were only eyewitnesses of His power. But when the day of Pentecost came, they were more than eyewitnesses—they possessed power themselves, and they experienced His divine presence personally. It was different from when Christ was with them. Nowhere does it say in the Bible that that the presence of God was reserved for the disciples alone, as if they were some kind of elite band.

Peter said, *"The promise is to you and to your children, and to all who are afar off, as many as the Lord our God will call"* (Acts 2:39). He quoted the promise from the prophet Joel, where God said: *"I will pour out My Spirit on all flesh"* (verse 17). This promise was not just for the day of Pentecost but for generations of those who would come to know Christ. It is part of the Christian experience.

If you haven't been filled with the power of the Holy Spirit, which is called "the baptism of the Holy Spirit," then all you have to do is ask. Luke 11:13 says, *"If you then, being evil, know how to give good gifts to your children, how much more will your heavenly Father give the Holy Spirit to those who ask Him!"* Power up by being filled with the Holy Spirit!

> ### Prayer:
> Lord, help me show to others the cross of Christ and the power of the Holy Spirit in my life. Jesus, your abiding presence dwells in me and is with me, as your Word says, forever (John 14:16). Thank you!! Thank you for continuing to lead me and guide me in your will. Thank you for allowing me to follow the Holy Spirit's leading in all things at all times. In Jesus's name, amen.

The promise is to you and your children and to all who are afar off, as many as the Lord our God will call. —Acts 2:39

Day 63

Resurrected to New Life in Christ

"For if we have been united together in the likeness of His death, certainly we also shall be in the likeness of His resurrection, knowing this, that our old man was crucified with Him, that the body of sin might be done away with, that we should no longer be slaves of sin. For he who has died has been freed from sin. Now if we died with Christ, we believe that we shall also live with Him, knowing that Christ, having been raised from the dead, dies no more. Death no longer has dominion over Him. For the death that He died, He died to sin once for all; but the life that He lives, He lives to God. Likewise, you also, reckon yourselves to be dead indeed to sin, but alive to God in Christ Jesus our Lord."
—Romans 6:5-11

LET'S LIVE THE RESURRECTED life, not the fallen, earthy life, embracing sin as something cool and cultural. That stuff put Jesus on the cross! Remember where God has now positioned you in Christ Jesus. Ephesians 2:6 says, *"....and raised us up together and made us sit together in the heavenly places in Christ Jesus."* Live your life according to your new position. Live not according to the dictates of your flesh but in accordance with God's will, as a reigning king with Jesus!

Galatians 5:16 tells us, *"I say then: Walk in the Spirit, and you shall not fulfill the lust of the flesh."*

Simply ask the Holy Spirit to help you live the way that God wants you to live. Power up by asking Him to help you overcome any situation that you're struggling with today.

Psalm 54:4 says, *"Behold, God is my helper...."* And John 14:16–17 says, *"And I will pray the Father, and He will give you another Helper, that He may abide with you forever—the Spirit of truth, whom the world cannot receive, because it neither sees Him nor knows Him; but you know Him, for He dwells with you and will be in you."*

Your position in Christ guarantees that your purpose and plans, given to you by God, will be successful. It won't happen overnight, but it will happen.

Prayer:

What an amazing promise you have given us in the resurrected Christ! To be dead to sin and *alive* to God! Father, show me what that means and how to live in that remarkable Truth. Thank you that the Spirit that raised Christ from the dead and dwells in me. Thank you that I *can* live a resurrected life, in Jesus's name! Thank you, Lord, amen.

Day 64

Good vs. Evil

"Abhor what is evil. Cling to what is good."
—Romans 12:9b

TO *ABHOR* **MEANS TO** detest and to turn away from what is evil; to *cling* means to stick like glue and to keep company with what is good.

In our society today, we are seeing people call good evil and evil good. It is the clashing of spiritual warfare, the kingdom of light vs. the kingdom of darkness. In these last days, those who stand for evil will mock, verbally attack, and alienate those who stand and live for what is morally and scripturally good. Psalm 38:19–20 (NLT) says, *"I have many aggressive enemies; they hate me without reason. They repay me evil for good and oppose me for pursuing good."*

In 3 John 1:11 (NLT), we are admonished to follow what is good: *"Dear friend, don't let this bad example influence you. Follow only what is good. Remember that those who do good prove that they are God's children and those who do evil prove that they do not know God."*

Remember, every day we are faced with choices between good and evil. Go with the good, and make sure the good is be aligned with God's

Word. The price you will pay to side with evil is greater and more horrible in the end than you can ever imagine. Evil can easily disguise itself as good, but if you know the Word of God and have a relationship with the Holy Spirit, you'll be safe. Discernment is one of your greatest blessings. Power up by praying always for discernment, and don't hang with evil!

"Do not be deceived: Evil company corrupts good habits."
—1 Corinthians 15:33

Prayer:

Heavenly Father, you warn me constantly in your Word so I will choose good over evil. And now that your seed — the incorruptible Word— abides in me, I have the power to walk after what is good and not give in to temptations of evil. Thank you for your righteousness that you have ascribed to me in Christ. Arrest me, Holy Spirit, when I turn toward an evil way. Give me discernment and convict me. My desire is to walk in your ways! In Jesus's name, amen.

The price you will pay to side with evil is greater and more horrible in the end than you can ever imagine.

Day 65

Only Jesus Can Change a Heart

"In this the children of God and the children of the devil are manifest: Whoever does not practice righteousness is not of God, nor is he who does not love his brother. For this is the message that you heard from the beginning, that we should love one another, not as Cain who was of the wicked one and murdered his brother. And why did he murder him? Because his works were evil and his brother's righteous."
—1 John 3:10-12

RACISM, HATRED, AND MURDER are birthed in the heart from one source—the devil! John 8:44 tells us this: *"You are of your father the devil, and the desires of your father you want to do. He was a murderer from the beginning, and does not stand in the truth, because there is no truth in him. When he speaks a lie, he speaks from his own resources, for he is a liar and the father of it."*

"Whoever hates his brother is a murderer, and you know that no murderer has eternal life abiding in him."
—1 John 3:15

Love is the opposite of racism, hatred, and murder. Love is of God because God *is* love. This is why the Church of Jesus Christ has been given the Commission to tell the world about the only solution to all the racism, hate and murder: Jesus Christ! Do the evil actions of people of all races make us angry? Yes. However, the Bible commands us to be angry but to sin not!

Ephesians 4:26–27 tells us, *"Be angry, and do not sin": do not let the sun go down on your wrath, nor give place to the devil."* If people who are not saved see us responding the way they do in anger with no resolve, then our Gospel and salvation are not relevant to them. But if they see us dealing with our anger through forgiveness and prayer, then they see Jesus in us.

People are looking for answers, and Christians have the Answer. When will we awake and start sharing Jesus with every person of every age?

Before you start making accusations and throwing stones on social media, ask yourself, "When was the last time I shared Jesus with someone?" Only Jesus can turn a heart of hate into a heart of love! Use social media to share the Good News of the Gospel. Use the Scriptures to express and apply God's Truth to every issue you address, not your opinions.

Power up by replacing racism, hatred, and murder with love!

Prayer:

Father, my heart is grieved when I see what is around me, in my nation and the world. Help me be part of the solution, not part of the problem. Keep my heart in your love. Help me see others and love others like you do. Give me boldness to proclaim your love through Jesus Christ to a lost world. In Jesus's name, amen.

Day 66

Unity Brings the Blessing

"Behold, how good and how pleasant it is
For brethren to dwell together in unity!
It is like the precious oil upon the head,
Running down on the beard,
The beard of Aaron,
Running down on the edge of his garments.
It is like the dew of Hermon,
Descending upon the mountains of Zion;
For there the Lord commanded the blessing—
Life forevermore."
—Psalm 133

GOD IS FOR UNITY, while the devil is for division. Unity is power and strength, while division is weakness and brings defeat. The devil promotes strife, conflict, competition, discord, dissension, fighting, quarrels, unforgiveness, and rivalry. This empowers the kingdom of darkness to try to divide and defeat us. The devil brings doubts into our minds to cause us to be double-minded (divided-minded) and to question God's Word.

What is the root cause of division? The passage in 1 Corinthians 3:3 answers this for us: *"For you are still carnal. For where there are envy, strife, and divisions among you, are you not carnal and behaving like mere men?"* To be carnally minded is to be selfish-minded—"it's all about me." The reason that many marriages end in divorce is selfishness—not willing to yield or serve one another.

The devil works hard to get us to operate by the flesh and promote pride, envy, and jealousy. He brings offenses into our lives to divide us. But God's Spirit promotes unity because in unity, we cannot be defeated! Don't let the devil win in your home or church. Power up by walking in love, forgiveness, humility, and unity! You'll see and experience God's life like never before; He bestows His blessings in unity.

Prayer:

Father, I thank you that you empower me, by your Holy Spirit, to walk in unity, not by the flesh. You said that if I walk by the Spirit, I will not fulfill the desires of my flesh. Teach me, more and more, to walk by the Spirit. I throw off the old man with his deeds and clothe myself in Christ. Thank you that you have made it possible, through your cross, to live in unity with my brothers and sisters. You have broken down every wall of division by the Cross. Thank you, Father. In Jesus's name, amen.

Day 67

Enduring Faith

"...who, being the brightness of His glory and the express image of His person, and upholding all things by the word of His power, when He had by Himself purged our sins, sat down at the right hand of the Majesty on high..."
—Hebrews 1:3

NOTICE THAT, IN THE middle of the verse above, it states, *"...upholding all things by the word of His power."* The word "upholding" means enduring. And yes, you can endure things successfully only by applying the Word of God to your issues or circumstances. It's the Word of God, in my heart and coming out of my mouth that enables me to walk through, deal with, and eventually experience victory over all issues! The Book of Psalms is a declaration of who God is in every tough issue and a declarations of His promises in every trial we face.

To endure, you must be rooted and grounded in the Word of His Power and continue to go forward because of His strength and power within you. If you continue to endure, continue to stand on, and consistently declare His Word, the outcome will be great!

"Indeed we count them blessed who endure. You have heard of the perseverance of Job and seen the end intended by the Lord—that the Lord is very compassionate and merciful."
—James 5:11

We find the power to endure by relying on the Spirit of Grace, who is the Holy Spirit within you. The Holy Spirit will empower you with His strength to endure through any situation until you see God's deliverance. Don't give up—instead, power up! When you fall, get back up, stay in the fight, and advance forward!

Prayer:

Dear God, thank you for the power of your Word that helps me endure every test and trial. There are many times in the midst of the battle that I grow weary and tired, and find it hard to endure further. I pray for your power to uphold me when these times come. I know that you are an ever-present help in trouble, and when I call, you will answer! Thank you, that I continue to persevere until I see victory! In Jesus's name, amen.

You can endure things successfully only by applying the Word of God to your issues or circumstances.

Day 68

The Power of Your Words

"Let the words of my mouth and the meditation of my heart be acceptable in Your sight, O Lord, my strength and my Redeemer."
—Psalm 19:14

JESUS SAID IN MATTHEW 12:34, *"Out of the abundance of your heart the mouth speaks."* This is why we must renew our minds, daily, to the Word of God. If we say words that are not acceptable to God, the kingdom of darkness can use those words to bring destruction to our lives and to people we love.

Proverbs 18:21 declares the power of your words: *"Death and Life are in the power of the tongue."* If you don't like the harvest in your life, change the seeds you're planting—your words!

Matthew 13:23 says, *"But he who received seed on the good ground is he who hears the word and understands it, who indeed bears fruit and produces: some a hundredfold, some sixty, some thirty."*

Negative thoughts will come, but you have control of whether or not you speak them out. Rebuke thoughts that are contrary to God's Word, and speak His Word. Power up by planting the Word in your heart in abundance! Pray what David prayed in Psalm 141:3: *"Set a guard, O Lord, over my mouth; Keep watch over the door of my lips."*

> ### Prayer:
> Lord, Your Words are so vital to every success and victory in my life. At times, I deal with situations in my flesh, and the words of my mouth are opposite of yours. Please forgive me and help me, Holy Spirit, to stop in any situation and listen for your Word over that situation. I renounce negative words I have spoken about (*list those things you think of*). I pray that you will break their hold in that situation, in Jesus's name. I replace them with your Word, God, which never fails. In the name of Jesus, amen.

If you don't like the harvest in your life, change the seeds you're planting.

Day 69

Walk the Path of Wisdom

"Do not enter the path of the wicked, and do not walk in the way of evil.
Avoid it, do not travel on it; Turn away from it and pass on."
—Proverbs 4:14–15

EVERY DAY, WE ARE faced with some sort of temptation that will lead us down the wrong path or endeavor to get us off the path we are on with God. In 1 Corinthians 15:33, we are advised, *"Do not be deceived: Evil company corrupts good habits."*

If we desire to be accepted and liked by everyone, it will be easy to get off the path that Jesus has for us. One path leads to blessing, but with it comes persecution at times. The other path leads to darkness, destruction, and disappointment—at all times.

Matthew 7:13–14 (NLT) clarifies this for us: *"You can enter God's Kingdom only through the narrow gate. The highway to hell is broad, and its gate is wide for the many who choose that way. But the gateway to life is very narrow and the road is difficult, and only a few ever find it."*

The reason the gate entry and path are so narrow is because Jesus is the only Way to the Father, and the Word of God is the only Way for us to regulate our lives. The devil offers many ways and paths, but all lead to eventual destruction. Satan uses people to tempt us to wander off the path that God has us on. Don't allow anyone to lead you to another path, no matter how many people are on it! Power up by staying on the right path—His path!

Proverbs 4:11–13 instructs us: *"I have taught you in the way of wisdom; I have led you in right paths. When you walk, your steps will not be hindered, and when you run, you will not stumble. Take firm hold of instruction, do not let go; Keep her, for she is your life."*

"But the path of the righteous is like the shining sun that shines ever brighter unto the perfect day."
—Proverbs 4:18

Prayer:

Father, I thank you for your wisdom and insight that keep me from the path of destruction. I thank you that you continually teach me and instruct me in the way I should go. You counsel me and guide me with your eye! (Ps.32:8) Your Word is a light for my path, and you ordain my steps. I pray for your continued direction in my life that will keep me on your path, for my desire is for you! In Jesus's name, amen.

Day 70

What Are You Feeding On?

*"Jesus said to them, 'My food is to do the will of Him who
sent Me and to completely finish His work.'"*
—John 4:34 (AMP)

FOLLOWING HIS WILL SHOULD be our ultimate goal in everything we do. His Word is His revealed written will to us today. God's Word is God speaking to us. The more you know His Word, the more you will recognize His voice. Our top priority is to renew our minds (thinking) so that our will is in harmony with His will. Do we have the power to carry out and accomplish His will? Philippians 2:13 says, *"For it is God who works in you both to will and to do for His good pleasure."*

"And do not be conformed to this world [any longer with its superficial values and customs], but be transformed and progressively changed [as you mature spiritually] by the renewing of your mind [focusing on godly values and ethical attitudes], so that you may prove [for yourselves] what the will of God is, that which is good and acceptable and perfect [in His plan and purpose for you]."
—Romans 12:2 (AMP)

"The world is passing away, and with it its lusts [the shameful pursuits and ungodly longings]; but the one who does the will of God and carries out His purposes lives forever. Feed on His Word, do His will, and you'll have good success and fulfillment in life."
—1 John 2:17 (AMP)

Power up by studying His Word and listening for His voice!

> ### *Prayer:*
> Father, I am so grateful for your Word and its power to transform my thinking and my doing. I pray to be a faithful disciple who hungers for your Word and makes it my food—not only hearing and speaking it, but *doing* it. I pray you will mold me more and more into the image of Christ so that my will may confirm to His. In Jesus's name, amen.

Our top priority is to renew our minds (thinking) so our will is in harmony with His will.

Day 71

The Poison of Unforgiveness

"And if he sins against you seven times in a day, and seven times in a day returns to you, saying, 'I repent,' you shall forgive him."
—Luke 17:4

IVING A LIFE OF unforgiveness is like driving a car with your emergency brake on—it's a lot of resistance to your destiny. You slow down and lose momentum. Deep-seated bitterness in your life eats away at your peace of mind like a deadly disease, destroying purpose and vision of life. In fact, there are few things as terrible to behold as the person who has harbored bitterness and hatred for many years. Never forsake forgiveness or the opportunity to forgive. When you live a life of unforgiveness, revenge naturally follows. But revenge is the deception of the devil. It might look sweet, but it is bitter. It always costs more to avenge a wrong than to release it and forgive.

Jesus commanded us to forgive. Forgiveness is really your deepest need and highest achievement. You'll never feel like forgiving because the flesh always wants revenge. Romans 8:6 instructs us: *"For to be carnally minded is death, but to be spiritually minded is life and peace."* Forgiveness is by faith and obedience to God—not something we do when we feel like it! We walk by faith, not by our feelings.

So, if you want to go the distance in your life and finish your race, all your envy, jealousy, unforgiveness, revenge, and fear must go. Without forgiveness, life is miserable and is regulated by an endless cycle of resentment and retaliation. What a dreadful waste of time that only ends in disappointment and depression! Your mind will be tormented, and your physical body will experience sickness and disease.

Power up by allowing the Holy Spirit to help you forgive like God forgave you! What was done to you might be inexcusable, but the sins God forgave you of were also inexcusable. Still, He forgave you through His Son's death and resurrection. Choose peace and life, walk in forgiveness, and don't let the devil give the offense back to you. Tell him that you have forgiven, and if he wants to bring it up again, go talk to God because you have given your unforgiveness to Him once and for all.

Prayer:

Father, when I realize all that I have been forgiven, my heart is overwhelmed with gratitude! Thank you. But at times, it is hard to do the same for others, especially those who have caused me pain. But I know that you love them as you love me, and there is freedom in forgiveness. I repent of unforgiveness toward others (*say their names out loud*). I choose to forgive in the same way you have forgiven me. Thank you for setting my heart free from resentment and for healing every broken place in my heart as I release my grudges, resentment, envy, jealousy, revenge, and fear. In Jesus's name, amen.

Day 72

When You Want to Give In and Give Up, Do This!

"Because your words are my deepest delight, I didn't give up when all else was lost.
I can never forget the profound revelations you've taught me,
for they have kept me alive more than once."
—Psalm 119:92–93 (TPT)

SOMETIMES, IT WILL SEEM like you have lost things in certain seasons of your life—and maybe you really have. But if you hold on to the revelations of God's Word and encourage yourself based on His love and promises, you will be able to recover what the enemy stole.

There was a time in King David's life when he made some bad decisions that allowed the enemy to steal that which was precious to him. He went directly to the Lord, repented, and prayed. His heart was filled with God's promises, and He went to God based on what was in his heart— the Word of God. Here was God's answer, from 1 Samuel 30:8: *"So David inquired of the LORD, saying, 'Shall I pursue this troop? Shall I overtake them?' And He answered him, 'Pursue, for you shall surely overtake them and without fail recover all.'"*

In Proverbs 4:21–22 (TPT), the Bible tells us to drink in God's Word: *"Fill your thoughts with my words until they penetrate deep into your spirit. Then, as you unwrap my words, they will impart true life and radiant health into the very core of your being."*

Why is this so important? Because the enemy will put thoughts in your mind that are contrary to God's Word. He knows that the more you fill your mind and heart with God's Word, the more you will declare His promises and that God will fulfill His Word. The enemy will turn up the heat and fire those negative words toward you. When that happens, take the sword of the Spirit and cut those negative words to pieces. Power up! Keep declaring and believing God's Word. Keep going!

Prayer:

Father, at times I have allowed negative words to get me to a place of wanting to give up. Discouragement, at times, can invade my resolve and make me want to give in to pressure and trials. But I thank you that your Word is my sword against the enemy. I wield it in Jesus's name! I cast down all the vain imaginations and bring them into obedience to Christ and the Word of God. Thank you that you uphold all things by the Word of your power, including me! I pray in the name of Jesus, amen.

"Because your words are my deepest delight, I didn't give up when all else was lost." —Psalm 119: 92 (TPT)

Day 73

Rise Up and Be Who God Has Called You to Be

"...to the intent that now the manifold wisdom of God might be made known by the church to the principalities and powers in the heavenly places, according to the eternal purpose which He accomplished in Christ Jesus our Lord."
—Ephesians 3:10-11

WHEN WILL THE CHURCH of Jesus Christ wake up, arise, put on our armor, get back to spiritual warfare, and be who God called us to be? We know where attacks come from. Revelation 12:12 (KJV) tells us, *"Therefore rejoice ye heavens, and ye that dwell in them. Woe to the inhibitors of the earth and of the sea! For the devil is come down unto you, having great wrath, because he knoweth that he hath but a short time."*

But does this mean that we are helpless or that we should sit around with our heads in the sand, waiting for Jesus to return? Should we imitate the prevailing culture and try to be like unbelievers? *No!* We are the light and salt of this Earth. We are the army of God, endued with His power, and we have the keys to the Kingdom. We are the intercessors, the warriors!

> *"So truth fails,*
> *And he who departs from evil makes himself a prey.*
> *Then the* LORD *saw it, and it displeased Him*
> *That there was no justice.*
> *He saw that there was no man,*
> *And wondered that there was no intercessor;*
> *Therefore His own arm brought salvation for Him;*
> *And His own righteousness, it sustained Him."*
> —Isaiah 59:15–16

Why aren't our prayer meetings packed ? We see the devil acting like he's in control, having it his way. Why are some pastors more interested in numbers, worried about not offending anyone, trying to build a reputation, and creating their own image by forsaking the demonstration of the power of the Holy Spirit? Some act like the lukewarm Laodicean church and forsake the fight of faith by refusing to engage in spiritual warfare like the tribe of Ephraim.

Psalm 78:9 says, *"The children of Ephraim, being armed and carrying bows, turned back in the day of battle."* No! If we do not get serious about intercession and get back to Kingdom business, this could happen in our families, churches, cities, and nation. *Wake up!* Power up!

> *"And do this, knowing the time, that now it is high time to awake*
> *out of sleep; for now, our salvation is nearer than when we first*
> *believed. The night is far spent, the day is at hand. Therefore, let us*
> *cast off the works of darkness, and let us put on the armor of light."*
> —Romans 13:11–12

Prayer:

Father, forgive me for being complacent and afraid as I see the world growing darker. I arise from my slumber and take up my spiritual bow and sword of the Spirit, which is the Word of God, and I advance! You train my hands for war and my fingers for battle (Ps. 144:1). This battle is not with flesh and blood but with spiritual wickedness in high places (Eph. 6: 12). You have given me authority over all the power of the enemy! I lift the banner of the victory of Jesus and forge forward in the day of battle, knowing that you have already won. In Jesus's name, amen.

Day 74

You Are the Light

"Do everything without complaining and arguing, so that no one can criticize you. Live clean, innocent lives as children of God, shining like bright lights in a world full of crooked and perverse people."
—Philippians 2:14–15 (NLT)

WE WHO ARE CALLED Christians are the "light of Christ" in this world. Seeing real Christians is to see the true reality and life of Jesus. Are your life and lifestyle declaring the light of Jesus? Or have you window-tinted your life so people can't really see your light? *Tinted* means a color that is diluted and less than maximum purity. Don't tint your life. Power up by letting your light (behavior, conduct, actions, words) shine brightly for Jesus.

*"Arise, shine; For your light has come! And the glory of the L*ORD *is risen upon you. For behold, the darkness shall cover the earth, and deep darkness the people; But the L*ORD *will arise over you, And His glory will be seen upon you."*
—Isaiah 60:1–2

Notice that when deep darkness is in the land, the Lord arises, and His glory is seen! How does this happen today? Matthew 5:14–16 says, *"You are the light of the world. A city that is set on a hill cannot be hidden. Nor do they light a lamp and put it under a basket, but on a lampstand, and it gives light to all who are in the house. Let your light so shine before men, that they may see your good works and glorify your Father in heaven."*

Prayer:

Father, by your very Word, you have called us—the church and me as an individual—as your disciples, the light of the world, a city on a hill. Forgive me for the ways I've placed a bushel basket over my light and not allowed the true light that is Christ to shine. You have chosen me out of the world to walk with you, to declare who Jesus is—not just with my words, but the way I live my life. I yield my heart to the Holy Spirit as my Helper to walk out my calling and to be the light in this world. In Jesus's name, amen.

We, who are called Christians, are the "light of Christ" in this world.

Day 75

Got Faith?

WHICH DESCRIBES YOUR CHRISTIAN life—doubt or faith?

Doubt sees impossibilities;
–   faith sees possibilities.
Doubt listens to the voice of the spirit of fear;
–   faith confronts and casts out the spirit of fear.
Doubt sees the worst-case scenario;
–   faith sees God's promise and His faithfulness and
     believes the best.
Doubt sees only the darkness;
–   faith sees the Light dispelling the darkness.
Doubt dreads to move forward;
–   faith stands up, steps out, and advances.
Doubt questions God's Word
–   faith answers, "Yes and Amen" to God's Word.
Doubt calls it as it is with no hope;
–   faith calls those things that do not exist as though
     they did and, in hope, believes.
Doubt magnifies the problem;

–　　faith receives wisdom and understanding. When doubt magnifies the problem, faith declares the solution to that problem.

Doubt sees no way

–　　Faith declares, "Jesus is The Way, The Truth, The Life!"

Today, power up by feeding your faith and starving your doubts! (See Romans 10:17 and 2 Corinthians 4:13.)

> **Prayer:**
> Father, thank you that you have given me "the measure" of faith. Lord, I believe! Help me conquer my unbelief as I walk out the life of faith you have not only called me to, but given me all I need to overcome and walk in victory! In Jesus's name, amen.

Feed your faith, and starve your doubts.

Day 76

Faith in God Changes Everything

"I would have lost heart, unless I had believed that I would see the goodness of the LORD in the land of the living."
—Psalm 27:13

DO YOU EVER FEEL like giving up? Notice, it is a *feeling*. Negative thoughts bombard our minds, which causes our flesh to feel like quitting and to stop believing. King David went through the same type of mental attack. All of us face days of feeling sorry for ourselves, and we think we're the only ones facing this type of problem. We are not. 1 Peter 4:12 (NLT) says, *"Dear friends, don't be surprised at the fiery trials you are going through, as if something strange were happening to you."*

Sometimes, we are afraid to say anything to anyone about our circumstances because we think they will think that we are not spiritually strong or do not have enough faith. This is all conjured up in our heads. We must look at how David handled this fight of faith.

He could have lost heart because everything looked bleak and almost impossible, but he kept on believing. Believing in what? That he would see (continual expectation) the goodness of God while he was alive. He didn't know what day a turnaround would happen, but he knew that God would come through for him.

Don't give up, throw in the towel, or succumb to negative thoughts. The Bible calls these "lying vanities." The devil is a liar! Be of good courage today. Power up by believing you will see His answer and His goodness! Wait in faith, and He will strengthen you. Get yourself back up, and go forward. You're tough; let the roar of the Lion of Judah come out of you. "Watch out devil, guess who's back!" Micah 7:7–8 says, *"Therefore I will look to the LORD; I will wait for the God of my salvation; My God will hear me. Do not rejoice over me, my enemy; When I fall, I will arise; When I sit in darkness, The LORD will be a light to me."*

Have a glorious day rejoicing in what you believe you will see!

Prayer:

Lord, fill me with courage today, no matter what I face. Let faith arise in me to speak only Your Word and believe that I *will* see your goodness now in this life. Your Word is my life, my strength, and my victory! In Jesus's name, amen.

Day 77

Please Do Not Feed the Fears

"For God has not given us a spirit of fear, but power and of love and of a sound mind."
—2 Timothy 1:7

DO YOU KNOW THAT fear feeds itself? It's true. Fear is contagious and viral. Even one teeny drop of fear will beget several negative emotions: worry, mistrust, insecurity, and so on. Fear's babies look a little different from one another, but all have the same DNA.

Fear tries to pose as Truth by weaving all kinds of negative thoughts and feelings together to make a case for itself, as it did in Job 3:25 (MSG). In this passage, Job said, *"The worst of my fears has come true, what I've dreaded most has happened!"* Remember, fear is a spirit, so when fear tries to sink its claws in me, what am I to do? I John 4:18 (AMPC) gives us the answer: *"There is no fear in love; mature, well-formed love turns fear out of doors, casts and expels fear." "There is no fear in love [dread does not exist], but full-grown (complete, perfect) love turns fear out of doors and expels every trace of terror!"*

Rebuke, resist, and cast out the spirit of fear. Replace it with the Truth of God's Word. Power up by declaring God's promises! Displace the spirit of fear with the spirit of faith. In 2 Corinthians 4:13 (AMPC), we learn, *"Yet we have the same spirit of faith...I have believed, and therefore have I spoken..."*

What are you speaking—faith or fear? Do a daily checkup from the neck up!

Prayer:

Father, help me remember that my words have power, either of life or death. Set a guard over my mouth (Ps. 141:3) so I may speak and declare only the things that are in agreement with you! I know that my faith is built by your Word, in my heart and in my mouth. Help me, Father, align myself with hearing and speaking your Word in my life daily. In Jesus's name, amen.

Day 78

I Will Fear No Evil, for You Are with Me

"Then Caleb quieted the people before Moses, and said, 'Let us go up at once and take possession, for we are well able to overcome it.' But the men who had gone up with him said, 'We are not able to go up against the people, for they are stronger than we.' And they gave the children of Israel a bad report of the land."
—Numbers 13:30

UNBELIEF IGNITES FEAR, WHICH, in turn, erases the promises and power of God. Fear magnifies every danger, circumstance, problem, and difficulty. It fills the heart with discouragement, which infects the hearts of others with hopelessness and despair.

Faith, on the other hand, sees, embraces, and declares the promises of God, which activates and ignites the power of God. Faith sees every danger, circumstance, problem, and difficulty not as impossibilities but as possibilities for a new experience of God's faithfulness and blessing. Faith sees every issue, circumstance, and problem as a God-sized opportunity for God's glory and our eventual testimony.

Faith magnifies God in the presence of insurmountable odds. Faith fills the heart with courage and praise, which infects the hearts of others with hope and confidence! Power up by embracing unwavering faith in Him!

How are you looking at your situation? Through the eyes of faith or fear? Who or what are you magnifying? Those who fear the darkness have no idea how powerful the Light is and what the Light can do! You can't turn darkness off, but you can turn the Light on, and darkness will be dispelled!

> *"Your word is a lamp to my feet and a light to my path."*
> —Psalm 119:105

Advance and possess the promises of God. You are well able to overcome.

> ### *Prayer:*
> Father, thank you for the great and precious promises that you have given me. Bring them to my remembrance when I face obstacles that are bigger and stronger than me. Help me see all the "God possibilities" in every situation and to declare them in faith! In Jesus's name, amen.

Faith magnifies God in the presence of insurmountable odds.

Day 79

Sorry Looks Back, Worry Looks Around, Faith Looks Up

"Now faith is the substance of things hoped for, the evidence of things not seen."
—Hebrews 11:1

THE VERSE ABOVE IS not a definition but a description of how faith works. Faith is an established conviction, based on God's Word, concerning things not seen and a firm, settled expectation of what we're praying about that lines up with His will, which is His Word.

Hebrews 10:35–36 makes us this promise: *"Therefore do not cast away your confidence, which has great reward."* Verse 36, *"For you have need of endurance..."* Are you ready to give up on your prayers? You're just about to see your answer and breakthrough! Don't throw away your confidence in God and His Word. *Confidence* means to have full trust, belief in God's power and Word; boldness, courage, determination, being firm in what you believe.

Don't stop believing now! The fact that the devil has turned up the pressure means your answer is coming. Get bolder and louder! Power up by turning the pressure back on the devil. Speak the Word with your God-given authority.

Don't back down. Don't turn back. Don't go visit self-pity, but move forward, walk and declare faith, not fear. You will see why you're believing.

> ### *Prayer:*
> Holy God, give me boldness to stand firm when the pressure is on, and to *not* give up, no matter what it looks like. Strengthen me to hold tightly to your Word until I see what I am believing and hoping for. I trust you, Lord, that you will perfect all that concerns me in every situation I face (Ps. 138:8). In Jesus's name, amen.

Day 80

When Opposition Comes Knocking on Your Door

"For a great and effective door has opened to me, and there are many adversaries."
—1 Corinthians 16:9

OPPORTUNITIES AND OPEN DOORS are so exciting, but with those open doors, many times, there will be opposition. Opposition is always God's opportunity for great victories and blessings! There is a sleepless foe who seeks to obstruct, divide, hinder, oppose, and stop our advancement. Where great opportunity abounds, opposition is sure to start up as its antagonist.

But remember what God said about your foe in 1 Peter 5:9 (AMP): *Resist (oppose, withstand) him, knowing that you're not the only one he is trying to stop!!! Stand firm in faith and continue to advance." But resist him, be firm in your faith [against his attack—rooted, established, immovable], knowing that the same experiences of suffering are being experienced by your brothers and sisters throughout the world. [You do not suffer alone.]"*

In Acts 14:27, Paul calls the open door "a door of faith." Hosea 2:15

states, *"It is a door of hope in the Valley of Trouble."* Jesus said in John 10:7, 9, *"I am the door."*

Don't let opposition stop you. You must persist, continue steadfastly with purpose, go all the way, and endure tenaciously. Power up! Let the opposition fan the flames of your persistence. Don't lose your confidence; keep pressing on. You will win!

Today is your day! If God be *for* you, *who* can be against you? You are *more than a conqueror.* You're not a whiner or quitter; you're a child of the Living God, strong and victorious! Go forward, all you Gideons!

> ### *Prayer:*
> Lord, at times, I feel like Gideon; hiding and cowering when opposition comes. But, just like him, you have called me a "mighty man (woman) of valor" (Judg. 6:12). Just as you told him to go in strength (Judg. 6:14), I ask for your strength as I face obstacles to my advancement to not only walk through them but to come out on the other side, victorious! Thank you, Father, for your faithfulness to see me through every time. In Jesus's name, amen.

Day 81

Your Praise Is a Weapon

"Don't use foul (worthless) or abusive language. Let everything you say be good and helpful, so that your words will be an encouragement to those who hear them."
—Ephesians 4:29 (NLT)

COMPLAINING, GRUMBLING, AND MURMURING about your circumstances will guarantee that your present issues will continue to linger. The more you complain, the longer you remain! But when we pray and praise with thanksgiving in the midst of our circumstances, God will raise us up out of them and turn our bad into good.

Romans 12:21 (NLT) instructs us, *"Don't let evil conquer you, but conquer evil by doing good."* Complaining is evil, while prayer and praise are good. As Christians, we must address our circumstances differently than the world so they can see and hear that we're different. Offering prayer and praise, instead of complaining, testifies that we trust in the all-powerful God.

Our prayers and praises will end with a testimony! God inhabits our praises, and miracles are the result. Acts 16:25–26 is a testimony to the power of your praise, even in the darkest situation: *"Around midnight Paul and Silas were praying and singing hymns to God, and the other pris-*

oners were listening. Suddenly, there was a massive earthquake, and the prison was shaken to its foundations. All the doors immediately flew open, and the chains of every prisoner fell off!"

Power up! Repent of complaining. Start using the weapon of praise to declare the might and power of your God!

Prayer:

Father, first, forgive me for not speaking according to your Word. Circumstances have overwhelmed me, and I have allowed complaining and murmuring to come out of my mouth. But I turn away from fear and take up your Word, the sword of the Spirit, and praise as my weapon to defeat the enemy and bring victory to my situation. You are faithful and will inhabit my praises. Just like you did with Paul and Silas, you will break every chain and bring me freedom! In Jesus's name, amen.

The more you complain, the longer you remain!

Day 82

Who Is Your Confidence?

"The LORD is my light and my salvation; Whom shall I fear?
The LORD is the strength of my life;
Of whom shall I be afraid?
When the wicked came against me
To eat up my flesh, My enemies and foes, They stumbled and fell.
Though an army may encamp against me, My heart shall not fear;
Though war may rise against me,
In this I will be confident."
—Psalm 27:1–3

TO BE *CONFIDENT* MEANS to be full of trust, believing in the trustworthiness and reliability of something or someone, having no uncertainty about a person's power and abilities. My confidence is totally and completely in God! Are you confident in God's ability to get you out of every situation? Or do you question His awareness of your present dilemma or His timing to bring your expected results? God's timing is always perfect! Put your total confidence in Him; don't rely on the strength or wisdom of man. Power up by being confident in His plan for your life!

Psalm 118:8–9 says, *"It is better to trust in the Lord than to put confidence in man. It is better to trust in the Lord than to put confidence in princes."*

This psalm was David's declaration of his confidence in God. What is coming out of your heart and mouth? Make his declaration your declaration today. Know that God moves on behalf of those who put their trust in Him.

> ### *Prayer:*
> God, I praise you with my whole heart! Examine me, and reveal any places in my life where my trust in you is lacking. My heart's desire is to fully trust in you, no matter what I see or experience in this life. But there are times when I allow fear to overtake my heart, and my confidence wanes. In those times, remind me who you are and that your Word alone is what's true in every situation. Fill my heart with your Word and your praise! in Jesus's name, amen.

Day 83

Never Give Up

"Likewise, the Spirit also helps in our weaknesses. For we do not know what we should pray for as we ought, but the Spirit Himself makes intercession for us with groanings which cannot be uttered. Now He who searches the hearts knows what the mind of the Spirit is, because He makes intercession for the saints according to the will of God. And we know that all things work together for good to those who love God, to those who are the called according to His purpose."
—Romans 8:26-28

ALL THINGS WORKING TOGETHER for your good is dependent on your intercession concerning your situation. The moment you begin your intercession, the issue or circumstance you face has already been assigned an outcome.

Isaiah 46:9–10 tells us, *"Remember the former things of old, For I am God, and there is no other; I am God, and there is none like Me, declaring the end from the beginning, And from ancient times things that are not yet done, Saying, 'My counsel shall stand, And I will do all My pleasure.'"*

It is assigned to work out for good and to bring glory to God, regardless of the situation. Our part is to—with the grace, strength, endurance, perseverance, and power of the Holy Spirit—stand in continual faith with thanksgiving until we see the assigned outcome that will be for His glory and our testimony. Power up!

It's the time element that throws us off. Don't grow weary while doing good, for in due season, all will work out for your good. Don't lose heart! Nothing can separate you from the love of God.

> ### Prayer:
> Father, how can I lose if you are for me and nothing can separate me from your love? I can't! You have already gone before me to make sure the outcome is good and brings glory to you. Help me always remember, in every circumstance, whether it looks "good" or not, that you are working it out for my good and your glory. Let me continually see your handiwork in my life in every situation. Help me know that you're right there in the middle of it, working it out. In Jesus's name, amen.

Every issue or circumstance you face has already been assigned an outcome.

Day 84

Whether You Think You Can or Think You Can't...You're Right!

"For the weapons of our warfare are not carnal but mighty in God for pulling down strongholds, casting down arguments and every high thing that exalts itself against the knowledge of God, bringing every thought into captivity to the obedience of Christ."
—2 Corinthians 10:4-5

EVERY ACTION IS ROOTED in the thought that produced it. God tells us to take every thought captive that does not come into alignment with His Word and His will for our lives. Any thoughts that we do not take captive, rebuke, and cast down that are in complete opposition of God's Word will bring us into captivity. They will produce an action that will eventually bring us grief, or even destruction.

Therefore, your thoughts are going to make you or break you. Thoughts will advance or retard your spiritual growth. Wrong thinking produces negative behavior, while right thinking produces right behavior. Our behavior and actions are the result of what we think and meditate on daily. Jesus said, *"Out of the abundance of the heart the mouth speaks"* (Matt. 12:34).

Your actions and behavior come from the abundance of thoughts that *you* allow into your heart. Quit blaming others for your actions. Power up! Even though people can influence us, they can't make us do what they want us to do unless we yield ourselves to their influence. Take responsibility for your actions and behavior. Change your thinking by renewing your mind to God's Word. Be totally committed to obey God's Word, and start casting down every thought that is contrary to what God's Word says and to who you are in Christ.

Proverbs 23:7 says, *"As a man thinks in his heart, so is he."* If your starting point is negative thoughts, then you're starting in defeat. If your starting point is God's Word and you don't abandon it, then your starting point is victory. If you cast down those negative thoughts, meditate on God's Word, and endure, your outcome will be victory! You choose.

James 1:3-4 (AMP) says, *"Be assured that the testing of your faith [through experience] produces endurance [leading to spiritual maturity, and inner peace]. And let endurance have its perfect result and do a thorough work, so that you may be perfect and completely developed [in your faith], lacking in nothing."*

Prayer:

Father, at times, I become complacent with my thoughts, letting them run wild without casting them down. My life and faith have suffered because of it. Forgive me. Thank you, Holy Spirit, that you will continue to lead, guide, and quicken me when my thoughts become nonproductive and don't line up with Your Word. Lead me into all Truth, your Word, your ways, and your will. Help me cast down any thought to the contrary! In Jesus's name, amen.

Every action is rooted in the thought that produced it.

Day 85

Don't Shrink Back

"Then He arose and rebuked the wind, and said to the sea, 'Peace, be still!'
And the wind ceased and there was a great calm. But He said to them,
'Why are you so fearful? How is it that you have no faith?'"
—Mark 4:39-40

IF YOU STAY SILENT when the storms of life come, the storms will conquer you. Whatever you don't confront that is out of God's will for your life will leave you devastated. There is a time to pray and a time to speak in the authority that God has given to you through His Word and in the Name of Jesus. He wants you to power up!

Jesus didn't have time to call a prayer meeting. He knew danger was imminent, so He didn't remain silent. He didn't shrink back in fear; rather, He spoke with authority in faith. The devil was trying to kill Him and the disciples, but Jesus, by confronting and speaking to the storm, conquered! Romans 8:37 declares that we are more than conquerors. Mark 11:23 tells us Jesus declared that *"whoever says to this mountain"*; the word *says* in Greek, means "whoever says and keeps on saying." Keep speaking until you see results manifest. Don't give up, and don't stop. The storm was the people's mountain—Jesus spoke to it and rebuked it!

Are you speaking with authority today, confronting your storm (circumstances)? Or are you staying silent, shrinking back, and succumbing to your situation? His Word is all-powerful! Don't stop declaring, rebuking, and praising in the name of Jesus.

> ### *Prayer:*
> I will stand up in the authority of Jesus! Father, continue to teach me to live and walk in the authority you have given me through the finished work of Jesus. That authority is not based on me or my goodness but on the power of the Blood of Jesus and the Word of God. I stand up in that authority and speak to the mountains and the storms in my life. As I do, they flee! In Jesus's name, amen.

Day 86

God Is Always Working on Your Behalf

"And we know that all things work together for good to those who love God, to those who are the called according to His purpose."
—Romans 8:28

EMEMBER JOSEPH'S STORY? HE faced much adversity until Pharaoh called him out of the dungeon into the palace. I'm sure that, through it all, Joseph would question if God had forsaken him and was not listening to his prayers. I'm sure he battled against depression and felt totally abandoned and betrayed by his family, thinking his dream from God was, maybe, just an illusion. But God's timing is always based on His plans.

You will emerge victorious and will be blessed, but you must continue to stand in faith and be faithful. Don't give up or give in—instead, power up! Your faithfulness and endurance will be rewarded. Keep your praise going, and He will bring you out of your circumstance to bring you into a blessed position!

"Therefore do not cast away your confidence, which has great reward. For you have need of endurance, so that after you have done the will of God, you may receive the promise."
—Hebrews 10:35–36

> ### *Prayer:*
> Father, the assurance that you're always working for my good fills my heart with peace and praise! Thank you that no matter what I see or how long it takes, you are working constantly on my behalf, bringing my prayers and your will to pass in my life. You are so good! You are so faithful! I trust you and put my confidence in your Word and faithfulness. Thank you, Lord. In Jesus's name, amen.

God's timing is always based on His plans.

Day 87

You Will Rise Again

"For a righteous man *may fall seven times and rise again."*
—Proverbs 24:16

THE SCRIPTURE ABOVE SAYS, "…and rise again"! Just because we face tough situations that cause us to fall into hard times doesn't mean we have failed or that we are failures. You haven't failed until you give up and stop trying. The key is not to stay down, but rather to rise again and conquer, like the character Rocky Balboa did in the *Rocky* movies. Sure, we all get knocked down at times, but when that happens, we need to ask ourselves, "What did I learn?" And then it's time to get back up. The problem is not what is happening, but the way we view it and react to what is happening. Power up!

My reaction to every situation is produced by my thoughts in that moment. If my thoughts are negative, it will produce a defeatist and "give up" attitude, which will result in staying down and depression. Quit taking everything so personal. Realize that you will have tribulations, but you don't have to stay down. You're still *who* God says you are, regardless of *where* you are. You're an overcomer and more than a conqueror!

It's time to get back up, brush yourself off, pour on some healing oil, get past feeling sorry for yourself, and get up and go another round. If you don't give up, God will see that the situation will work out for your good. Come on, let the champion in you rise up and advance with a winning attitude! If God be for you…who can be against you?

> *"Do not rejoice over me, my enemy;*
> *When I fall, I will arise;*
> *When I sit in darkness,*
> *The LORD will be a light to me."*
> —Micah 7:8

Prayer:

God, your Word is full of promises and exhortation when I face situations that knock me down. And although these times hurt and can be hard, your promises lift me up, and I am encouraged. By your Word, I can rise; I can believe, and my attitude changes. Holy Spirit, speak your promises to my heart in this time; speak your strength and encouragement to me. The enemy may try to rejoice over me, but I am not utterly cast down, for you are with me. You will lead me into a broad place (Ps. 118:5) and set my feet on a solid rock—the solid Rock who is Christ! In Jesus's name, amen.

You haven't failed until you give up and stop trying.

Day 88

Down in the Dumps

"When my soul is in the dumps, I rehearse everything I know of you,
From Jordan depths to Hermon heights, including Mount Mizar."
—Psalm 42:6 (MSG)

WHEN IT SEEMS EVERYTHING is going in the opposite direction of my prayers and negative thoughts are harassing my mind, I begin to call to memory who God is to me and who I am to Him. I call to mind how great He is as my Father and all He has promised me as His son! My heart begins to soar like the eagle, and my mouth begins to roar like the Lion of Judah within me.

Put fear in the devil's camp today; let the world hear your roar! Power up by fixing your eyes on the love, grace, and mercy of God, and soon you'll be praising Him. Before you know it, you will explode with joy from deep within your soul! Come on and praise Him. You'll go from the dumps to the heights of joy. Put on the garment of praise, and drive the devil crazy!

Prayer:

Proclaim Psalm 149 out loud over your life and circumstances, as a prayer, and watch the enemy run!

"Praise the LORD! Sing to the Lord a new song,
and His praise in the assembly of saints.
Let Israel rejoice in their Maker;
Let the children of Zion be joyful in their King.
Let them praise His name with the dance;
Let them sing praises to Him with the timbrel and harp.
For the LORD takes pleasure in His people;
He will beautify the humble with salvation.
Let the saints be joyful in glory;
Let them sing aloud on their beds.
Let the high praises of God be in their mouth,
And a two-edged sword in their hand,
To execute vengeance on the nations,
And punishments on the peoples;
To bind their kings with chains,
And their nobles with fetters of iron;
To execute on them the written judgment—
This honor have all His saints."

Day 89

Praising God in the Eye of the Storm

*"You are a hiding place for me; You, L*ORD*, preserve me from trouble, you surround me with songs and shouts of deliverance. Selah [pause, and calmly think of that]!"*
—Psalm 32:7 (AMPC)

THE TRUE SIGN OF a true worshipper is the lack of complaining, griping, criticizing, fault-finding, pointing the finger of accusation, and murmuring, plus the consistent proclamation and praise of Truth in the face of every trial and adversity. The true worshipers worship in Spirit and Truth; therefore, the songs of deliverance are constantly surrounding them.

This is exactly what happened to Paul and Silas in Acts 16. They were severely beaten, totally misunderstood, treated with disrespect, and put in a prison. When your situation is unfavorable, tough, or out of your control, or when you're being mistreated or taken advantage of, or something is not your fault but you still get hurt and attacked by the enemies of your faith and your trust in God is being assaulted, how are you going to react? How are you reacting right now? The way you react will be a witness to others of your faith in God because they are listening to and watching you. Are you singing today or complaining? It's your choice. Power up! Pray and sing, and watch your miracle manifest!

"After beating them black and blue, they threw them into jail, telling the jail keeper to put them under heavy guard so there would be no chance of escape. He did just that—threw them into the maximum-security cell in the jail and clamped leg irons on them. Along about midnight, Paul and Silas were at prayer and singing a robust hymn to God. The other prisoners couldn't believe their ears. Then, without warning, a huge earthquake! The jailhouse tottered, every door flew open and all the prisoners were loose."
—Acts 16:23–26 (MSG)

Prayer:

Father, I worship you! In the midst of my trouble, I lift up my voice and my hands to declare that *you are victorious*! To declare that your hand will do valiantly (Ps. 108:13) in this fight, that the battle is not mine but yours, and that you are a mighty man of war (Ex. 15:3)! You will not forsake me in my trouble but are with me in the midst of it to bring deliverance. Therefore, I sing a song of deliverance today in thanksgiving of what you are doing and about to do to show yourself strong on my behalf (2 Chron. 16:9)! In Jesus's name, amen.

Day 90

A New Season Is Coming!

"For there is hope for a tree,
If it is cut down, that it will sprout again,
And that its tender shoots will not cease.
Though its root may grow old in the earth,
And its stump may die in the ground,
Yet at the scent of water it will bud
And bring forth branches like a plant."
—Job 14:7–9

SO MANY PEOPLE SEE their lives like a tree that has been cut down, with no hope for the future. But look at His Word—there *is* hope! Because you have roots in God, at the scent of water (a metaphor for the Holy Spirit), rivers of water are flowing out of your very inner being. The moment His presence begins to manifest and you begin drinking from the water of His Word, new life will begin to appear!

A new season is about to emerge; new buds are ready to appear. Jeremiah 1:11–12 (AMP) says, *"The word of the LORD came to me, saying, 'Jeremiah, what do you see?' And I said, 'I see the branch of an almond tree.' Then the LORD said to me, 'You have seen well, for I am [actively] watching over My word to fulfill it.'"* The almond tree was known as the "awake tree" because it was the first tree to bud in the new year (late January). It was the symbol of watchfulness.

Don't give up. Reawaken to a new beginning! A new season with new opportunities and possibilities is ready to spring forth. Start singing a new song of praise, and stop listening to and singing the blues. Power up through His word and prayer!

Psalm 92:12–15 tells us, *"The righteous shall flourish like a palm tree, He shall grow like a cedar in Lebanon. Those who are planted in the house of the LORD shall flourish in the courts of our God. They shall still bear fruit in old age; They shall be fresh and flourishing, to declare that the LORD is upright; He is my rock, and there is no unrighteousness in Him."*

Meditate on these Scriptures.

Prayer:

Father, it seems like I have been feeling cut down for so long. I have reached a place of fruitlessness and am striving in my own strength to make branches grow. Thank you for your promise of new growth and new life! Thank you for your faithfulness to perform in my life what you have promised. I look forward to the days ahead with hope and praise of a new season. I praise you and thank you! In Jesus's name, amen.

A new season is about to appear; new buds are ready to appear.

IF YOU'RE A FAN OF THIS BOOK, WILL YOU HELP ME SPREAD THE WORD?

There are several ways you can help me get the word out about the message of this book...

- Post a 5-Star review on Amazon.
- Write about the book on your Facebook, Twitter, Instagram, LinkedIn, – any social media you regularly use!
- If you blog, consider referencing the book, or publishing an excerpt from the book with a link back to my website. You have my permission to do this as long as you provide proper credit and backlinks.
- Recommend the book to friends – word-of-mouth is still the most effective form of advertising.
- Purchase additional copies to give away as gifts.

The best way to connect is by visiting www.mycl.church